MENTORS

RUSSELL BRAND

MENTORS

HOW TO HELP AND BE HELPED

HENRY HOLT AND COMPANY

NEW YORK

Henry Holt and Company
Publishers since 1866
175 Fifth Avenue
New York, New York 10010
www.henryholt.com

Henry Holt ® and ® are registered trademarks of
Macmillan Publishing Group, LLC.

Library of Congress Cataloging-in-Publication Data

Names: Brand, Russell, author.
Title: Mentors : how to help and be helped / Russell Brand.
Description: First Edition. | New York : Henry Holt, [2019]
Identifiers: LCCN 2018060283 | ISBN 9781250226273 (hardcover)
Subjects: LCSH: Mentoring. | Self-help techniques.
Classification: LCC BF637.M45 B73 2019 | DDC 158.3—dc23
LC record available at https://lccn.loc.gov/2018060283

Our books may be purchased in bulk for promotional, educational, or
business use. Please contact your local bookseller or the Macmillan Corporate
and Premium Sales Department at (800) 221-7945, extension 5442, or
by e-mail at MacmillanSpecialMarkets@macmillan.com.

First US Edition 2019
Published in the UK by Bluebird, an imprint of Pan Macmillan
Designed and typeset by Andrew Barron @ Thextension

Printed in the United States of America

1 3 5 7 9 10 8 6 4 2

For my daughters

———

CONTENTS

INTRODUCTION

Have you ever heard Brian Cox or any other particle physics genius (they're ten a penny after all!) describing the vastness of our universe? The likelihood that even beyond its fathomless reach are more and more, likely an infinity, of universes? When I, with my blunt intellect, fondle these imponderables I feel suspended between awe and despair. Within the infinite all forms of measurement become meaningless as they can only refer to parochial patterns; time and the laws of physics only local customs in our universal village.

When I hear Cox speaking of Carl Sagan, however, the giant star of astronomy who inspired the then adolescent scientist, I feel held between awe and hope. Sagan was a mentor to Cox. Although they never met, Sagan functioned as a mental symbol, a target, a role model that the younger man could emulate on his own journey to greatness.

A hero is an emblem that demonstrates the possibility of inner drives becoming manifest. It could be John Lennon, whose journey from ordinariness to greatness, from glamour to domesticity, from grandeur to humility provides coordinates to others who want to undertake a comparable journey. It might be Amma, the Indian teacher and mystic whose certainty of God's love has generated profound social change across Asia. Her devotion has inspired others through philanthropic works to establish schools and build hospitals and homes. At first, of course though, she was dismissed as a mad teenage girl in a fishing village in Kerala going into trances and cuddling everyone. People thought she was nuts. Greatness looks like madness until it finds its context.

Mentorship is a thread that runs through my life, now in both directions. I have men and women that I turn to when the way ahead is not clear and younger people that look to me for guidance in their own crazy lives. Note that the mentor's role is not solely as a teacher, although teaching is of course a huge part of it. When Cox talks admiringly about Carl Sagan it is not just because of his academic exper-tise, it is because he felt personally guided by him. Watching Sagan's emotional take on science in *Cosmos*, was the trigger that made Cox, at twelve, decide to become a scientist.

We choose mentors throughout our lives, sometimes consciously, sometimes not, sometimes wisely, sometimes not. The point of this book is to understand this process and to improve it. When selecting a mentor we must be aware of what it is we want from them. When we are selected as a mentor we must know what the role entails. One of the unex-pected advantages that my drug addiction granted me is that the 12 Step process of recovery that I practise includes a mentorship tradition.

When you enter a 12 Step program, you have to ask someone else to guide you through the steps, or 'sponsor' you. This typically induces an unwitting humility; few people would say 'Hey, babe, it's your lucky day – I want you to take me on a spiritual journey.' Usually one feels a little shy on asking someone to sponsor them, a little meek, a bit like you're asking them on a date. In undertaking this we accept that our previous methods have failed, that we need help, that our own opinions are inferior to the wisdom of the mentor and hopefully the creed that they belong to. In 12 Step custom the sponsor teaches the sponsee the method by which they practised the 12 Steps; they replace their own sponsor, and they give to another what they have been given. Whilst it may bear personal inflections, it is sufficiently faithful to the original program to inhere its power. The same, I note, is true in martial arts traditions, there's a lineage and a system that is carried from teacher to student. Clearly there are parallels in academia, but anyone who's been to school knows that mass education can be pretty inconsistent and the average harried educator has too many bureaucratic and financial burdens to mindfully endow more than a handful of pupils with the elixir of mentorship.

In this book I will talk to you about my mentors, how they have enhanced my life in practical and esoteric, obvious and unusual ways, by showing me that it is possible to become the person I want to be in spite of the inner and outer obstacles I face. I will encourage you to find mentors of your own and explain how you may better use the ones you already have. Furthermore I will tell you about my experience mentoring others and how invaluable that has been on my ongoing journey to self-acceptance, and how it has helped me to transform from a bewildered and volatile vagabond to a (mostly) present and (usually) focused husband and father.

I have mentors in every area of my life: as a comic, a dad, a recovering drug addict, a spiritual being and as a man who believes that we, as individuals and the great globe itself, are works in progress and that through a chain of mentorship – and the collaborative evolution of systems – we can improve individually and globally, together.

Sometimes in my live shows I ask the audience if they belong to any groups: a football team, a religious group, a union, a book club, a housing committee, rowing club – I am surprised by how few people have a tribe. Whilst the impact of globalization on national identity cannot yet be fully understood, I can certainly appreciate the reductive appeal of statist myth. I become ultra English during a World Cup, the last one in particular was like a jolly revival of the 'death of Diana' in its ability to pull a nation together in collective hysteria. But soon enough the bunting comes down, the screens in public squares go black and we are atomized once more. The space between us no longer filled with chants, ditties and 'in jokes', eyes back on the pavement, attention drawn within. I'm not suggesting the deep alienation that Late Capitalism engenders can be rinsed away by joining a bowling club, but it's a start, and having a teacher within the group to which you belong provides intimacy and purpose. In the guru traditions of India the love between teacher and student surpasses all other forms, for here it is explicit that what is being transferred in this relationship is nothing short of God's love and how an individual can embody the divine.

We live in lonely and polarized times, where many of us feel lost and fractured. It is evident in our politics but political events reflect deeper and more personal truths. I've been trying for a while now to explain what I feel is happening in the societies that I'm familiar with, by which I mean Europe, Australia, the United States – not that I'm claiming to be a sociologist, I don't have a clue how to approach whatever the hell may be happening in Pakistan or China, but here, here in our post-secular edge lands where the old ideas are dying and the new ones not yet born, I feel a consistent and recognizable yearning for meaning beyond the dayglow ashes of burnt-out consumerism, lurching dumb zombie nationalism, starchy, corrupt religion and the CGI circus of modern mainstream media. I've been watching for a long time and I knew before Trump, Brexit, radicalism and the 'new right' that something serious was up. You know it too. Sometimes we despair and sometimes we distract because it seems like too much for one person to tackle and we've forgotten how to collude. Yet alone I am nothing.

CHAPTER ONE

AMONG LOST BOYS: THE TIME BEFORE MENTORS

No one escapes childhood unscarred. The raw animalism is crudely sculpted by events and best intentions. Drives designed to survive and thrive in a world we have long concreted over thrash against screens and surge with sugar. And now in practice, as a dad, my tender sentimentalism is tested by the iron will of a toddler – 'I'll nurture that wild and perfect spirit' at 3 a.m. becomes 'Oh God. Oh dear Lord, make this fucking child go to sleep'. Does anyone cross as vast a terrain as the Rousseauian idealist turned parent? If a conservative is a mugged liberal, a dad is a knackered Jesus.

No child is awake enough to appoint a mentor, you take what you are given; it isn't until adolescence that we grope beyond the boundaries of Mum & Dad, or whoever was doing that job. Some boys give that job to peers in gangs, some girls give it to ponies but, for all of us, beyond these narrow roles are scores of Ben Kenobis and Maya Angelous just dying to pass on a lifetime of twinkling wisdom. Worth noting that if the teen craving for an idol is soaked up by vapid consumerism, all that hormonal good intent could get splurged on a digital Kardashian or wrung out on a beatboxing pipkin in a backward baseball cap. Yes, yes, the adolescent wants coitus but what does the wanting want?

Our glacial days of digital perennialism place us in a constant 'now' without ever really being present, and icons are torn apart. No sooner does a hero rise than she is exposed as a hypocrite. Malcolm X was a rent boy, Gandhi had some odd nocturnal habits and even Che, the obligatory teen portal into rebellious sentience, was a homophobic murderer. Too Much Information; the iconoclasm of our omniscient but omni-dumb days unweaves the carpets that we may have walked upon and leaves us in the wasteland of the 'only human'.

Before I was awake to such things as conscious mentorship, I adored my older cousins and they begat Morrissey, who shone the torch of adulation on Jimmy Dean and Oscar Wilde. Each retains a place in the 'constellation of self' as I blaze into my middle years. My cousins with their chip-toothed Essex cool, Moz's elevation of suffering, Dean's sexy damage, and Wilde is a little too complex to skip over with a handful of adjectives but, God, the tragedy, the wit, the ambiguity, the social conscience and the contradiction.

We make ourselves, consciously or unconsciously, building patterns in the infinite, holding on to strands amidst the limitless, sometimes grasping through fear, sometimes clutching with desire. Through proper mentorship, a transition of skills, a nurture of energy can take place that instantiates an adult from the beautiful wreckage of childhood, a sober man from the drunk, a master from the student, a mother from the girl.

When I was sixteen I left home in search of my misfor-
tune and quickly found it. It was in Bermondsey. There's
enough misery in South London for everyone, it wasn't as
cool then as it's meant to be now. There I holed up with
some Lost Boys, two years older and a great deal wiser, and
in my mind I made them legends. When I look back now at
these eighteen-year-old lads I see that they were herberts but
I needed them to be cool, so cool is what I saw. Question: is
there an objective 'reality' or a series of interdependent
mental projections? In other words, was Hitler a kind of
nationally conjured totem to re-energize castrated and
enraged Germany? Were The Beatles a quadrant of awakening shamans that carried a generation from plodding rock,
to sexy pop, then psychedelia and ultimately consumerism?
The events in the outer world are governed by subtler energies, many of which pass through our collective psyche. No
doubt meteors and hurricanes shape environment but
culture, by definition, is the manifestation of human drives.
There are patterns, shapes and archetypes that recur.

At nineteen when I first saw the already dead Bill Hicks
I felt a bodily transference. I'm not claiming to be entitled to
the mantle of the great American stand-up, there's enough
people doing that, but I felt empowered and inspired by him.
Inspired – he put breath into me. And breath is life. It is
curious to me that in early life my mentors were remote.

Famous or dead or both. It wasn't until Chip Somers that I chose to emulate another man in order to move from one state to another.

CHAPTER TWO

THE FIRST MENTOR: INITIATION WITH A DEVOTED ATHEIST

A recovering drug addict is a contradiction by definition and Chip is a fine example. A nerd bank robber. Middle-class scum. Pious atheist. I didn't make him a mentor when he diagnosed my addiction, at that point he was just the bloke who ran the treatment centre I was unwillingly being packed off to, someone I'd have to charm into letting me out at some point. For all I knew there would be a test and a certificate. In fact there was: drug tests and a kind of 'well done, you' certificate – like 'Sports Day Medals for Everyone' at a progressive school.

When I met Chip he had been clean for a little longer than I have now, sixteen years. He'd been trawling London with zealous do-goodery, interfering in the life of Davina McCall and was friends with Eric Clapton, so he had credentials. Of course I was not famous at this time but if you'd cut me open I was pure ambition. Well, not pure, I was significantly contaminated with crack and heroin – that was the problem.

Chip had been a far worse drug addict than I was. For one thing he was intravenous, for another he served real time for proper crime; in the warped ecology of junkies and inhabitants of the underworld that means he had status. More practically it meant I could trust him on the subject of addiction and the business of quitting drugs.

In this case there was the added advantage that I had been institutionalized and that there was a clear endpoint in mind – abstinence – and a method to achieve it: 12 Step recovery. Perhaps these are the perfect conditions for mentorship: a mentor, a mentee, a method and an institute. The Hindu guru–disciple relationship typically functions along these lines, as does martial arts training. Interestingly, neither of these paths have an obvious western counterpart; the most obvious comparison – trade apprenticeship – is contextualized by commerce and professional necessity. In my experience, mentorship is more successful when there is no financial component.

The most immediate and obvious thing that Chip taught me was that it is okay to talk about your feelings, more than okay, mandatory. In fact that's all we did, talked about feeling vulnerable, inadequate, fearful and angry. Honesty is non-negotiable in a relationship of this nature because you need to trust someone if you're going to allow them to help you, and they of course need to be dealing with the truth of who you are, not the Facebook, press-release version of yourself you've been fobbing the world off with up till now. Through his honesty, Chip demonstrated that it was safe to be vulnerable; through his own abstinence and change he showed me that the task I had to undertake – to give up drugs and alcohol – was entirely achievable and he told me what I would have to do. What I brought to the relationship, I now know, was Honesty, Open-mindedness and Willingness – known as

'HOW' in 12 Step jargon. This is the attitude I deploy still in any relationship where I am the student. Whether in meditation, Jiu Jitsu or business affairs I approach my teacher, my 'mentor', in an honest, open-minded and willing way. I recognize that they have something I want, that they have achieved something that I haven't, that as I am in the moment I sit before them, I am insufficient, and for the transfer of energy or education to take place I must be mentally and spiritually prepared. This is as true for a yoga class as it is for a Spanish lesson or therapy.

No wonder my high school education was a washout. On the days I showed up I sat detached, glum, angry and impenetrable. I did not want what the teachers had to offer, I wanted to go home. But to be fair to teenage me, because I've learned to love that little guy, while the schools I went to may have declared that they were there to educate, they were in fact, unconsciously or otherwise, there to indoctrinate their charges into a state of malleability and passivity. Generally educational bodies do not exist to bring out your innate brilliance but to monger your wayward nature into a unit of manageable energy that will not be too disruptive to the social systems that benefit the powerful.

Chip was not about that at all. He was a kind and caring man, it was clear to me – even then – that he felt invested in my wellbeing. In the intervening years I have changed so much that it is hard to recall the vulnerability I felt then or how alien Chip's kindness was.

In the three months that I was in treatment I was given written tasks to complete that were formulated around the first three of the 12 Steps:

1. Admit you have a problem.
2. Believe in the possibility of change.
3. Ask for help and follow suggestion.

In practice this meant providing accounts of when my drinking and drug use put me in danger or caused me to behave regrettably, examples of new habits I could adopt to support change, and ways in which I could get help that weren't previously available.

Nearly sixteen years later I use this formula when dealing with less critical problems of my own, and when mentoring other people. It is a near universal template. Having Chip as a witness and a guide as I undertook this as a novice was invaluable. When I gave accounts of the conse-quences of my drug use he was non-judgemental and offered stories of his own. He was able to validate ideas I had about how to change my habits and patterns and suggest better ones; and, importantly, he was a living demonstration of the success of the methods. He was also the first person that I was able to ask for help in a way that felt safe and free from hidden or unclear obligation. This is the first, and in a way most vivid, example of mentorship because the intention was so explicit, transition from drug user to abstinence; the method was established, the 12 Steps; and the environment supportive, a treatment centre for addiction. This meant that the relationship between Chip and myself had a good chance of succeeding as long as I was honest, open and willing, was able to accept my own flaws, believe I could change and give Chip the authority to steward that change. His obvious compassion, humour, honesty and experience meant that my decision to trust him felt safe. When I read my life story to him, a common therapeutic exercise which gives your mentor an idea of your version of events and forces you to commit yourself to a narrative, he said, and I remember this most vividly and it still elicits a little, inward shudder, 'Poor, lonely, little boy.'

Hearing him say that made me feel understood but humbled, like I no longer needed to inflict an impression of myself on others, that I was no longer required to dupe or trick people into accepting a version of me that I constructed as I went along. It kind of winded me. It meant that I could accept that my shameful feeling about being that little boy could be addressed head on. It meant that I could tell Chip saw the truth in what I wrote. My mate Matt read the same life story the night before I handed it in, he'd come to visit me in treatment, rather sweetly. Let me tell you his assessment of the work was less sympathetic, he wrung it out for comedy in the most brutal fashion, cruelly pointing out my unconscious attempt to present my life as a kind of rock 'n' roll bio, scoffing at the bits where I 'lived above pubs', and coldly undermining the self-aggrandizing tone. Humbling in another way. For this reason I have peers, to remind me where the boundaries of my tribe lie. But if I want to get beyond these boundaries I will need a mentor. Chip didn't take the piss. It would've been pretty unforgivable if he had (!). He saw past all the posturing and grandeur to the deeper truth; I was an uninitiated man and I needed to be recognized and encouraged.

The mentorship Chip gave me was a success, and the goal of every student is to surpass the master. I may never have achieved this goal but I did become clean; once clean I could resume my all-consuming quest for glory and with that I was alone once more, untethered, fatherless. The encoded individualism runs so deep in me that once the obvious symptoms of addiction had been addressed, its power re-asserted, and for a decade I was lost in rudderless indulgence and illusion. Whilst I had learned from Chip how to become drug free, I had failed to learn a deeper lesson.

CHAPTER THREE

———

MENTOR TWO: ZEN NURTURE FROM THE WISE WOMAN

A divorce is a rupture, the deliberate detonation of a bond made in good faith, a shared and mutual dream. The bouquets, the invites, the napkins, the fucking napkins, all torn up and undone. That happy ceremonial day and pink-cheeked love will be fastidiously unpicked, but first the explosion of divorce. Slowly it has been dawning that things are not working, your own limitations and the limitations of the person you married swarm and enclose like locusts feasting on the corpse of goodwill. They were not who you thought they were, you are not who you think you are. The tracks that led uninterrupted to the future of total union are wrenched up and mangled, the blissful plains you had land-scaped together are gone and there is a steep drop into the gawping nowhere.

Now, in the aftermath of the split, I am with Meredith in the modest room in North London in which she practises. It is here and there festooned with Zen Japanese art and books on Chinese medicine. I suppose she is in her fifties but I've known her over ten years and she's always seemed to be in her fifties. She is American, an acupuncturist, calm, sharp and smart, warm in unexpected starts. I must've told her of my plan to cope with the pain of divorce by having sex with lots of people because she said, 'What does it mean then, all this meditation, this program, this faith in God, if as soon as there is a problem in your life you turn to sex?'

Well, what it means is that the meditation, program and faith in God are all phoney, hollow practices, phatic chants and empty dances that I carry out when the going is good, basically just for their aesthetic value. But when pain comes, and pain is always coming, I will abruptly turn, like a good little soldier, to a materialistic solution to a spiritual problem. It means that my true religion is materialism, my true god is the ego, and what I really mean when I say 'I want to be enlightened' is 'I want to feel nice'. It wasn't necessary for me to say this, and I didn't, but the question had revealed the hidden truth: that I still found it hard to live a spiritual life, particularly when threatened, and that is when you need the spiritual life the most.

Ostensibly Meredith is an acupuncturist; I went to see her with a bad back. I don't know when my back got better but I continued to go because the conversations we had during the acupuncture were, to me, more valuable than the acupuncture itself, which I feel somehow will appal her. Meredith is interested in deep truth, wisdom. She is a healer but carries none of the woo-woo baggage that term implies. Some time into our relationship it occurred to me that you have the family you are born with and the family you consciously appoint. Meredith became an appointed mother. I don't mean for this to diminish the vital role of my own mother, nor do I mean to say that I have depended on

Meredith to the enormous degree that the word 'mother' suggests. It is that on some biochemical or philosophical level I recognized her as a portal for maternal nurture of a type that I required as an adult. A mentor is a type of hero and a hero is a symbol, much of the work they do for you is in effect done by you, yourself, in your own mind. Take the example of Meredith and the revealing question she asked in this instance. She revealed to me that I was living dishonestly and demonstrated, by her own being, that there was an alter-native. Now I don't need to set up camp at the foot of her bed or be there at the breakfast table sobbing, while she feeds her actual family, to receive the benefits of her wisdom. I just need to be open to education, willing to change. In this way we author our reality.

I determined to make Meredith a 'mother'. I decided to accept her nurture. This is a more conscious and less severe example of mentorship than I experienced with Chip, my requirements had changed. Whilst I still have a long road ahead of me and evidently at the time of Meredith's searing question I was still unconsciously functioning through addictive behaviour – distraction from pain through sex – I'd grown beyond the point of shuffling dependency. Any good mentor will enhance your self-sufficiency.

Meredith became a mentor because her words held weight. I'd lie there supine and pinned listening to her talk about Lao-Tze, Zen, the Dao, the *I Ching*, Caravaggio, Michelangelo, R. D. Laing, parenthood, everything. I'd natter back and enquire, I'd follow up on her suggestions, take a trip to Rome, do a course in Religion and Global Politics. The things she talked about were true, they helped, she was able to teach and connect. Obviously a teacher must convey information or techniques that they have mastered to a novice who, by definition, can only partially appreciate what they're saying. They have to live in two worlds at the same time, the wisdom and the innocence. Perhaps in this is the connection between the teacher and the shaman; the shaman moves between worlds, dimensions, levels of consciousness and returns from kingdoms unknown with treasure for the community.

Meredith would come to my flat sometimes to treat me when I was all entangled in fame. Often I'd keep her waiting while I scampered about on the phone or canoodled. When I arrived in the room I'd find her in silent meditation, apparently untroubled by my lateness. Sometimes she comes to my shows and her insights are always valuable, her comments are always exactly the feedback I require. She seems always to me to be asserting that truth is deep, that we must keep going, that truth is hard, that we cannot settle for the merely palatable. We must always keep burning through our illusions. When she speaks of Michelangelo or Caravaggio it's like she speaks to the universal, that there is a language in light, a perennial truth in the expressions of human faces, that the artist can capture, render, create truth. It is this that I need from her. The spiritual courage to keep looking, a hardness always couched in compassion, the mother's love but an acceptance of the duty we bear if we choose to walk the path. Do not stop, do not deceive yourself.

It took time to learn the lessons of my divorce, perhaps I am learning them still. My impulse to fall into addiction was a reminder of how close to destruction I reside. These teachers often appear at pivotal times, moments of transition, to help you along the path.

CHAPTER FOUR

MENTOR THREE:
THE GOODISON GURU

India, the land of the gurus where celebrity culture, such as it is, still refers to the template of reverence that easy pagan idolatry affords. Gurus adorn tea towels and mugs like Kardashians. When Yogananda describes the first sighting of his guru, to a westerner the sincerity of his adulation is almost obscene. We only love so wholeheartedly and uncynically in adolescence, or when we revisit that hormonal tundra in juvenile adulthood. I was in my own storm of idiocy, my own adolescence beaten thinly almost into middle age, on a trip with a woman who I blindly adored, who I had ill-advisedly appointed as a custodian of my heart – one last throw of the dice. We who look for god in romance are doomed. Your idol will fall and you will be too bereft to pick up the pieces.

After a disastrous holiday where the delusion we had impulsively projected shattered and left just the bare bones and broken hearts of us, I ran into Jimmy in an Indian airport. I knew Jimmy Mulville already, he works in TV and he doesn't drink, like me. I'd once overheard him say, 'I wanted to live an autobiography, not a life,' and instinctively plagiarized it in my own autobiography. He was with his wife and three of his four children navigating an airport. I was at the carousel with my paramour conducting an introduction with the stink of argument still on us. Later on in the flight, Jimmy ambled over and gave me a book he was reading, Robert Johnson's *Inner Gold* – a Jungian account of mentorship, how we 'give another our gold to carry or hold'. Gold in this metaphor being, I suppose, a symbol of our highest self, our truest intention, the aspect of us that is so beautiful it is too much for us to hold alone.

I took the occasion of our meeting – a time when my old idea of salvation through romantic love was demonstrably failing – the location, an airport, and the book, on mentorship, to be a sufficiently serendipitous spur to ask Jimmy to mentor me. What I knew of him then was: he is a successful producer and manager of people, he has been married for over twenty years, he's been alcohol and drug free for over twenty years, he's from a working-class background, he supports Everton FC, he's an only child, he has a dark side, he is funny, he's educated, both classically – he went to Cambridge on a scholarship – and in the 'school of hard knocks' sense. Asking someone to mentor you, as I have said, is a simultaneous acknowledgement of vulnerability and admiration, and even in the most secular and occidental context bears a trace of Yogananda's euphoric sincerity. No one wants to be rejected by someone they admire and who knows they're vulnerable. But after my holiday my old method of redemption through love was still giving me a good battering. If you'd asked me at the time what the problem was, I would have instantly blamed the woman I was going out with. Now I know the problem was my unreasonable, unconscious requirements.

I asked Jimmy for help, he agreed to help me. I told him about the melee that was my relationship and he was always able to 'hold it'. Meaning that my problems never fazed him – the last thing you need when opening up your heart is for the person you've appointed to blanch or gag. He pointedly never offers unsolicited advice, instead meeting my enquiries with his own experience. There is a great power in this. Some of the things he has said landed as perfectly in my mind as the first maxim of his I plagiarized: 'Being Human, is a "me too" business, we're all in the mud together' or 'Next time you see the signpost that points in the direction of a destructive relationship, don't go in that direction.'

Jimmy guided me. Not only through the conclusion of that clearly doomed relationship but also helped me to let go of the many co-dependent professional relationships and friendships in which I was mired. Co-dependency can mean 'relationships where the boundaries are not clear and the roles are blurred'. In my case I had outsourced many aspects of my life that I needed to take personal responsibility for. This is likely particularly common in showbusiness, where there is an industry built on the indolent whimsy of the 'artist'. Through Jimmy I saw there was no future in that identity, that I had made myself dependent on too many people because I was afraid to grow up. That I selected relationships with women that were doomed because I was trying to satisfy a religious impulse in a practical dynamic. A marriage must be clear and robust, the married couple must have a mutual vision of the relationship and a consensus on their roles within it. It is a highly practical arrangement that includes domestic management, sex, child-rearing, recreation, counselling, tension, friction, love and hate. I used to enter into relationships with abandon, like it was a balmy lagoon. I was always astonished by the tsunamis and whirlpools that consumed me. I now know that instead of appointing a female to make me feel complete, I must access the 'female' aspect of myself and honour that – this means an open relationship with my creativity, my emotions and my wildness. Certainly not an open relationship of any other description. We've had that argument let me tell you.

To give you one clear and Damascene example, recently I awoke in County Wicklow knowing, deeply knowing, that I must go for the daybreak swim that I'd agreed to go on, that I could not lie in bed next to my wife all cosy, I had to whip off the duvet and get in the car and drive to Greystones, where the other dawn swimmers would be. Stephen Flynn, one of identical twins of the Happy Pear ethical eatery, had invited me and when I said 'yes' I was pretty sure I was lying. But when I awoke I knew I must go, that in the cold and perfect morning, in the novelty of the trip with these Irish strangers, I would find something in myself that I would otherwise be trying to drag out of my wife. I foresaw the dawn and the crashing tide, the tentative strangers that dive from the rocks into cold morning. I stopped my idle mind and rose against its decree and let my mad freewheeling beast of a dog into the passenger seat like Chewbacca. It was still dark. In the car I felt my soul rewarded, I felt alive. I felt I'd broken free of the trammels of my own making. It was of course beautiful there. Stephen Flynn and his brother are men on the path and we must walk with those who walk the path with us, or we feel so terribly alone.

Those twins – even when you're just with one of them – are a handful, male but gentle and kind, even the bravado is endearing. Down to the Greystone rocks we go, past the abandoned edifice of the eerie Victorian hotel that looms over the ladies' bathing beach, as was. On we go to a jutting peninsula that reaches into the orange glinting morning. There they are, this morning crew, with hot drinks and warm smiles, a tribe intuitively formed around the totem of the dawn swim, its obvious root in hunting and worship and the deep gods of nature. I refuse of course to dive from the mad, serrated, Tetris block that Stephen suggests but jump in from a lower ledge – 'Don't kill yourself trying to impress strangers, Russell, it's not 1999,' says some wise and tutored inner me. Bear swims too and it's quite a morning and I feel certain in the breaking day that God is everywhere.

Jimmy, like Chip, is an atheist. But he lives like a holy man, by which I mean, as if the real world is the unseen world, the eternal world, not the temporal one. He goes on annual trips with the teacher who taught him Classics as a kid because he missed a school trip to the ancient world. His now elderly former teacher leads him through Athens or Pompeii giving the man the lessons he would have given the boy. I asked him why he makes this pilgrimage and he said it connected him to the person he was.

I sometimes find that when we reach across the dualistic divides there was no boundary there at all. I've already seen that the male and female effortlessly coalesce and are found, the one within the other. In my conversations with great atheists I've found spiritual reverence that borders on shamanism. As Yanis Varoufakis, the principled Syriza beefcake who led Greece's democratic revolution, said: 'Some people believe that matter preceded spirit, others that spirit preceded matter – I happen to believe the former. In any event, spirit is here now and we have to deal with it.' He made this lucid announcement while I interviewed him for my podcast, *Under the Skin*. Whether you are an atheist, believing that we are naught but gas and maths with no intelligence or consciousness beyond what's required to access bananas, or you believe that the phenomenon of consciousness itself is evidence of a connection to something beyond the material, we have to now agree that morality, kindness and love are present in our deepest codes.

Mentorship needn't be total duplication. I'm not trying to become my mentors, I'm using them as a focal point to help me summon and nurture latent qualities which, without stewardship, I may not be able to realize. At the point I met Jimmy I was trapped in a pattern, behavioural and mental, that I bet a neurologist would be able to point to on a thermal screen. Well-worn circuits. Because I identified with aspects of his past and wanted to emulate him I was willing to ask him for help and then accept that his insight would be of more value than my own instincts and experience.

We met at a point that was transitional, in my own life but also so typical that it is well covered in myth and mocked in popular culture as a 'mid-life crisis'. I was confronted with a choice between my old way of doing things, which on the surface looked like promiscuity, hedonism and obsession but was in fact a romantic, root-less belief that an idealized woman could save me or that many women could distract me. I'm not saying I was condi-tioned or even programmed into believing those ideas but both of them happen to be popular cultural notions – woman as redeemer and the male as hunter, or to use the parlance of the day, player. I could've continued to search for an earthbound goddess or ambled into middle life still acting like a seventeen-year-old but something deep within me called out for change.

Alone, I am not at all convinced that I would have been able to break this cycle, the pain would've led to seeking the balm of the very behaviour that caused it – addiction in an instant. Because I have a program of recovery I recognize that I must when in crisis:

1. Acknowledge it.
2. Believe it could improve.
3. Ask for help.

You'll notice I continually paraphrase this simple formula as it is a tool that can be relied upon to instigate change in any circumstance. In my book *Recovery*, where I break down the 12 Steps in detail, I spoke at length about mentors, their pivotal role in instantiating new psychic energies – this is as clear an example as I can offer.

In my moment of crisis after my relationship with this extraordinary but unsuitable woman ended, a woman who in fact had the essential qualities of every girl I've ever loved from the playgrounds of Grays, Essex, to the red carpets of Los Angeles, a kind of unobtainable helix of mystery and destruction (not objectively, I mean in conjunction with the ridiculous mix of hormones and behaviours wrapped in the bag of skin I live in – one man's Delilah is another man's soulmate), I felt that not only had that relationship failed but that my whole life had failed. In a way I was right; I had recognized the relationship as an emblem of my poor navigational skills that had led to the rocks I was dashed upon. Even if the truth hadn't risen to my conscious mind as wisdom, it was present in my belly as misery.

Jimmy, when I rang him, forlorn in the aftermath of this wreckage, was unflustered. I said I could walk away from everything in my life, that none of it seemed valuable or real. That I didn't want to live in the house I lived in, do the work I did, hang with the people I was working with or even wear my clothes anymore. I may not have said I felt like I was dying, or that I wanted to die, something I continually announced in my actual adolescence; I was constantly poised, bread knife at the wrist in some dreadful tableau of self-sacrifice, bawling at my baffled mother that I wanted to die. Of course, then there was no one who could 'hold' that truth: that was, in fact, the problem.

Jimmy was unfazed when confronted with the middle-aged version of the suicidal teenager. Firstly he is not emotionally involved. The care, or even love, he feels for me is not going to capsize his objectivity, he is a father figure, not a father. A father can be, as we all fucking know (!), a more fraught and conflicted role. Being an appropriate mentor, somewhat delivered by serendipity – all my mentors have floated into my life, like celestial beings – Jimmy knew what to say. He had been in this position himself. It is normal, necessary, beneficial to, at the midpoint in the journey, question the direction of travel. The relationship was but one aspect of my life that needed to change, it was the most vivid and obvious but it was merely the emissary for all necessary change. I had been living in an illusion and the illusion was fading. I was awakening from the dream of my previous self and if the somnambulance was roughly disrupted I would not withstand the shock.

I will always remember the tone with which Jimmy spoke if not all of the content. He normalized my feelings, he contextualized them, he told me they would pass and that this was part of my metamorphosis. Crucially there was an authenticity to his words that meant I trusted him more than my own feelings. He always demonstrates these qualities. When I make the pilgrimage to his Camden office and patiently wait while he wraps up a meeting or a call, I sit on the leather sofa, self-conscious and reverential, focused on the picture of Duvall and Brando in *The Godfather* that is above the sofa opposite, above where he will sit. He is good humoured and bursting with tales of work and family, expletives and comic voices, sometimes deep sentiment. His classical education means that his counsel is spiked with references to Ovid or Virgil and I sometimes want to take notes but that may prevent me from continually taking note.

Whilst it is tempting to idealize him I am aware, due mostly to the authenticity of our communication but also because I'm not twelve, that he is flawed and complicated and imperfect. This is important: the nature of our relationship is bounded. I am not dealing with the total of this man. Is one ever dealing with a total person? I am dealing with him in his role as a mentor. He is an ideal to which I aspire and an objective voice when I need guidance. There is no value in iconoclastically demolishing my personal Olympus, in destructively slobbering over Martin Luther King's infidelities. I focus on the components of my mentor that I am hoping to summons from myself, the dormant power that alone I may not activate. If I say, 'Well, Jimmy isn't perfect,' I will ultimately use the ordinary details of human fallibility to impair my own progress.

Sometimes when I am making an incredible fuss over some minor piece of bullshit, when I am contemplating leaping out of my car like a slender James Gandolfini to confront someone at a traffic light, I think: 'Wow, there are men who call me up for advice and here I am, unable to contend with normal emotions – what a fraud I am.' But this is not the case, my all too evident flaws do not prevent me being a successful mentor as long as these relationships are correctly bounded. All of the people I mentor understand the nature of this dynamic, its benefits and its limitations. They know that the method I use is verified and ancient. They know that I want nothing from them, that my only intention is to help them; I don't want money, prestige or power from them. These are men like me, men that have turned to drugs and sex to cope with the absence of a spiritual dimension to their life. Who in the absence of loving guides have improvised philoso-phies from their primal urges and crazy circumstances. When they need me I am not the fool at the traffic lights, I am the man they need me to be.

Once I called Jim when he was about to take his seat at the theatre or something that meant there was little in the way of small talk, and though I was quietly frantic he dispatched insights like sharp, quick darts, for all I know while buying a box of Maltesers. Perhaps young men like me go awry because nobody can hold them. I don't mean embrace, I mean in a parental sense, like parentheses, to 'bracket' them, to stand as a dam either side of the wayward lash and unmovingly emit care. The only authority I ever knew was negative. Either inefficient or corrupt. This is the consequence of living with false ideals in a materialistic society. The authority that I give to Jimmy is sacred, I know he is flawed but I am not consulting with the flawed part of him I am consulting with the part of him that is willing in spite of his own numerous obligations, work, and family to provide loving counsel for free. I believe this relationship becomes a conduit for truth, divine truth. That needn't mean it's all chocolates and roses. There's a fair amount of 'suck it up' and 'face your fear', but it is truth. Perhaps we can take truth to mean the timeless, the universal. Things that will not erode and fade, qualities I need to live the life I have moved into.

How does someone who has never been a father become one? How do any of us progress beyond our temporary limits? The potential person we can become hums in an invisible grid within and without us. A genius may actuate by intuition but all of us need heroes, role models and mentors, that we may see what is possible, living mandalas to lock onto as we inhale and expand into new states.

CHAPTER FIVE

MENTOR FOUR: THE WARRIOR ON THE MAT

No personal expedition could be more intrepid and bold than my venture into combat sports. There in every precinct or forgettable town in unforgivable fonts are emporiums for fisticuffs, salons for stubbly cuddles and yet, at forty I had avoided them all. Sure, in Hollywood when living in yet another frat house, mad cabin of maleness, tended to by my female friends, so as not to live entirely without nurture, I would have an occasional well-mannered brute stop by and give me kid glove tutoring in 'hands on' machismo, but these visits were somehow ersatz and rootless. All forms of training without clear intention could suffer from a sense of unad-dressed futility; they are, after all, a kind of rehearsal, a play. A good martial arts instructor, though, will instil a 'realness' that alters the student's perspective. Not that all my teachers in those arid glistening hills were ineffective, one in particular was amazing, but prior to him there were a few stout Krav Maga fellas whose verbal description of the techniques they were teaching made me baulk and go giddy at their goriness, meaning I could of course never learn them – e.g. 'Put your thumb in their eye socket then run it round the rim and flip out the eyeball like a lychee.' I made that up, but it's very much the mood of Krav Maga. It's so vindictive, I'd have to be in a Liam Neeson-style calamity to even countenance it. A capoeira man, who looked like a lethal refugee from Milli Vanilli or a fire breather at a destination wedding, gave me and my suffering squad of Lost Boys such a vigorous work-out that one of our number didn't walk for days after and had the air of a man trapped in a painting, rigid behind a curtain, banished to a dimension he could only peer from.

Benny Urquidez, aka Benny the Jet – who I appointed to do some rough and tumble nannying in my time in the Hills – was the real deal. In appearance he had the leathery magnetism of Johnny Cash and a small gimlet-eyed face. He was demure and quiet and I could hear the faint beating of the war drum when I was with him. He had absorbed and could convey great wisdom. His fists were bunioned and tough. He once demonstrated a jab to the ribs that I'd had trouble mastering by delivering the blow to my flank by way of example. It was as if he were delivering a parcel from another world where the laws of thermodynamics didn't apply. How could such a small, sharp movement cause such precise profound pain?

Benny also taught me, and actually it shows what a great teacher he was because at the time I didn't question the apparent incongruity of this, a system of prayer that I use to this day. Basically the formula is:

1. Gratitude – 'What are you grateful for today?' Be specific and think of three examples.

2. Courage – 'Ask for courage and think where you will need to apply it over the course of the day.'

3. Healing – 'Pray for the healing of people who need it.' Specifically, this means whenever anyone tells me of hardship I remember them the next time I pray, if nothing else it disrupts the constant self-centred introspection.

4. Synchronicity – 'Ask to see the signs and guidance of the unseen world.' Now, when coincidences occur, I know I asked for them so I look to see if there is anything I can learn.

5. Alignment – 'Be in alignment with the Greater Will.' Don't be caught up solely in egoistic need, have purpose that benefits your real values.

I don't even know how we got on the subject of prayer. Perhaps he looked at my martial arts and thought, 'Bloody hell, this guy is gonna need some support from the cosmic forces that transcend our current understanding of the material world. Down with the gloves, onto the knees.'

During these cosseted dalliances with combat sport I knew I was cheerily placebo-ing myself, that whilst I could tick the box of martial arts training I was not going to become more effective as a result of those delightful, bizarre or torturous sessions.

I started to think seriously about Brazilian Jiu Jitsu (BJJ) because of Joe Rogan. I admire what he is doing with his online media and I respect his authenticity. It's quite hard for me to be objective about 'tough' men because I have never quite relinquished a kind of quiet, sexless, homoerotic intrigue when it comes to a bruiser. I'm actually a bit embarrassed by it but think it's kind of funny too. I would estimate that this attraction is a residual longing that focused mentorship will relieve or certainly affect. It's not that I 'fancy' these men, it's more that I want them to like me, which is perhaps an unconscious attempt to embody a presently unrealized energy. I like that Joe has built an empire based on his abilities and opinions without apparent compromise and has circumnavigated the many forces within media that homogenize and dilute the power of content providers. It seems logical to take at face value Joe's own assessment that martial arts have greatly contributed to the person he is. It makes sense to me. There is a grounded embodiment to him that I feel martial arts can deliver.

When I moved from city life to rural life three years ago, a conscious effort to ground and grow, my interest in combat sports was intuitively rekindled. Let me be clear, I'm living in a theme park version of the bucolic. I'm not drawing water from a well or wrestling sows for their titty-milk (which is the country way, I understand). Nevertheless, I have escaped the bluebottle blur of city life, an environment designed to maintain a constant level of anxiety syphoned periodically by entertainment. Here it is different, here I remain home, which I did in cities too, in a demented Travis Bickle-ish way, only popping out to scan the pavements for opportunities for knee-jerk vigilantism. I lived in an East End mews in the dog days. My nightlight was a street lamp that cast steep shadows in the unending stairwell of the vertical warehouse flat I occupied. In spite of the kudos of the cool postcode, the truth was by night people came to piss and do drugs on my doorstep as I clung to strangers and flinched. I forget this. I forget the misery of the inauthentic life, now that I am swaddled in cosiness and occasionally sigh at the loss of fleeting distraction.

Here as a father and a new man I understood I must rebuild myself. I took football lessons like a seven-year-old, fathering myself past the spilled barricades of the clumsy past. The lessons took place in a park with a twenty-five-year-old handsome lad called Charlie. He put out cones and everything. I kept it up for a while – the lessons, not the ball, I never mastered that – but these sessions in a rec were not what I really needed. I'd misdiagnosed the condition, plus I'm not Marty McFly scooting back to Sports Day to try and sneak a bronze. A few lads I met near where I live, blokes like me that don't drink, said there was a martial arts club, Genesis, nearby. A mad worshipper of synchronicity and signs like me will leap at the chance of attending a gym named after a book from the Bible. The more I think about it, the more ambitious a name I consider it to be: 'the dawn of new universes'; 'God and man in communion'. A bloke called Paul runs it. 'Why not call it Leviticus or Revelations?' one day I shall spuriously enquire. I went down there and as martial arts gyms go it wasn't bad. There is a certain uniformity: crash mats, rubber busts of a Dolph Lundgren-looking character that you're invited to pummel, the smell of inside a boxing glove, old vinegar, feet, genitals, rock or rap music – I suppose classical music, post Kubrick, would be worse – trophies and medals on a windowsill, not dusted, some group shots in a municipal hall, maybe some en-couraging slogans, and men, mostly men. A few women, yes, but mostly men.

Mentoring here becomes clear, instruction delivered by a teacher to students. There is a system, there is a space, a tradition, a church. At first I went to kickboxing classes, one on one, with real-life GI Joe (in appearance, mostly), Paul Busby, before beginning training with Brazilian Jiu Jitsu blackbelt Chris Cleere. Chris is not overtly garrulous or excessively communicative, there is, I might say, a degree of shyness. Not the blushing timidity of a twelve-year-old majorette, but the kind of male diffidence common in working-class men which could perhaps be seen as a lack of 'flashness', quietly 'matter of fact'. It is when practising Jiu Jitsu that his potent fluency is evident. A sharp and jagged flow of physical syntax as he anacondas you into submission with elegantly composed violence.

You arrive at the lesson with your 'gi' in a branded bag. The gi is, I suppose, a coarse pair of pyjamas, which in my case are never quite long enough and stop halfway down the shin. Putting on the gi is more ritualized than you might think and involves more complexity than an outfit comprising two parts ought. There is a drawstring around the waist of the pants that is needlessly convoluted, embedded in a tunnel of fabric, emerging at several interludes, on the sides and front and you're supposed to tighten it by sharply pulling the exposed side pieces then tying a bow – which seems an inappropriate word here – at the front. I've never fully under-stood this. The jacket is pretty simple but I bet there's a rule about which lapel goes in front that I've never learned, and the application of the belt is a martial art in itself. I once did a class with Rener Gracie and when he demo'd how the belt should be tied, by tying mine for me, like when a parent puts a tie on you, the concluding yank was so definitive I thought it would still be about my hips when I took to my grave. In truth the bloody things come undone about every forty or fifty seconds and you spend a good portion of any class retying them, which is, frankly, a relief.

I've never been in a more plainly stratified environment than a group BJJ class. The white belts dress at one end of the gym and the higher belts at the other. As far as I know this has never been legislated but it is fastidiously observed.

The end nearest the door with the mirrored wall is where the white belts gather. The far end of the room, where the kit is kept, is for the higher belts. The men stretch and change. The music and the buzzer that signifies the commencement and conclusion of rounds are controlled from that end of the room. BJJ is about control.

Genesis gym is on a trading estate in Marlow; Marlow is basically a lovely town on the River Thames. This is not a gym in Toxteth or Soweto, and the coffee shop downstairs is delightful. But there is something essential happening here. The dark-belted men (all men in this case) hang out like apes up the control end. Chris, of course, shaved head, fifty, a titanium skeleton of indefatigable Jiu Jitsu, and Dave, forty-five, latte coloured and fit. Once I examined (subtly) every visible part of his body and we are almost different genders, his hands as different from mine as mine from my daughter's. I imagined his arms on my body, replacing mine, not caressing – that's not where this is going, though I can see why you might have assumed that – and it would be like I was driving a forklift truck. Dave is a purple belt, known colloquially as 'Smasher' and on the few occasions I sparred against him it was like drowning in hard water. Not really worthy of the word sparring either, unless Hiroshima sparred with the atomic bomb. The others up the control end vary but usually include the handsome, unduly geeky Paul Busby. It was my wife who observed that there is an oft overlooked geekiness to martial artists because the nerdy component is obscured by a marzipan-thick layer of testosterone. Seldom though, in my experience of BJJ, the kind of prognathic machismo you'd find in an average boozer, I suppose because posturing is unnecessary when status is clearly marked and conflict so nakedly resolved.

Going to a one-to-one BJJ lesson is intimate. Whilst I consider myself quite a tactile man, I note that I like to be the initiator and dominator of social contact with men and I've never experienced the degree of closeness that BJJ requires. Even if you look at high-level MMA, much of it is basically ground-down erotica. Very easy to sexualize as an observer, not as a participant, the idea of getting an erection while under that kind of pressure is stupendous. I know nothing in this environment. In my relationship with Chris I am a total novice and completely vulnerable. The process by which knowledge of this type is taught is by demonstration and drilling. Usually on the floor, in a clinch, legs wrapped about the waist, grips to the collar and sleeve. There isn't much pain, the point of it is to get your opponent to submit, generally you submit before serious damage is rendered, but there is a lot of discomfort. For me, initially the discomfort was psychological, being willing to be pulled about, crushed and bent-up was difficult.

The reason I believe Chris is a great mentor, comparable to the people who have helped me psychologically and spiritually, is that his teaching is profoundly changing me, realizing and releasing dormant energy that I'd be incomplete without. This is a non-verbal education. Of course we talk, but the language of Jiu Jitsu is spoken by the body. It is highly cerebral, in that the strategic demand and the requirement to spot patterns are as important as speed or strength. If intelligence is the ability to spot patterns, then this is a highly intelligent game. It's like chess but with someone strangling you.

To become a black belt is hard and usually presumed to take ten years of dedicated training so Chris is highly accomplished yet is able to gently inculcate these specific and sometimes complicated moves in a way that makes sense. Jiu Jitsu, though, comes alive when the moves work in combination. This is experienced through drills, yes, but mostly sparring. In sparring there is a loss of self comparable to sex and surfing, where the relationship with the body is intense but relaxed and flowing rather than staccato. Don't get me wrong, the majority of my time sparring is spent dealing with a far superior opponent operating at ten per cent of their capacity, still crushing or folding me with relative ease. There are moments, though, where there is real awareness that Jiu Jitsu itself exists as an independent entity, an ideal, like an invisible grid in the cosmos, and we, through choreography, are able to embody its power. That through subjugation of the self we can channel the higher power of this force, and much of this seems plainly analogous to all that is important in life. The whole philosophy at times seems to be a tool for teaching life lessons. Like life, Jiu Jitsu is charged with moments of suffering and opportunity. There are times to be passive and times to be aggressive, times to explode and even times to surrender. This is not the kind of thing that Chris would pontificate on, but the manner of his teaching not only embodies these ideas but transmits them so that I am able to embody them too.

There is so much fear in my life. When all is well my mind drifts like iron filings to the magnetism of inevitability in the form of dark fantasy: 'Everything is okay now but think of all the things that could go wrong now you love so many people . . .' Sparring in Jiu Jitsu lances the fear of the future by being a real and embodied present. When someone is choking you and you know you must tap or go uncon-scious, it is a safe way of realizing the otherwise abstract fear of violence and violation.

One time, sparring with another white belt, I was choked out with a 'guillotine' choke, where one arm is round your head like a playground headlock and the other under your throat pulling upwards. Because it was another beginner, not Chris or another warlord from the control end of the room, the sparring was competitive and – this is interesting – my ego was suddenly invited back into the equation. When I'm sparring with Chris the relationship has explicit and implicit safety built into it, I'm not competing, I couldn't compete, I'm learning. When it's against Dave, Smasher, my ego would do just as well to pit itself against the hydraulic jaws of a garbage truck. Against another white belt, my ego sees a little chance for glory and sidles in where it would best be left out. As the choke took hold and I felt beaten and submitted it were as if the wrench on my neck had opened a valve to an inaccessible cellar where my bruised adolescent self lay hiding. I sat quietly afterwards, uncertain of what I felt. My wife remarked that I was quiet that evening and I, reluctantly (ego, again) told her what had happened. She almost thought it funny, not in a derisory way or in a way that made me feel more ashamed and defensive, but in a way that highlighted the idiosyncrasy of my feeling. I spoke about it to someone else who doesn't drink and does Jiu Jitsu and he explained that it's a contact sport and that these feelings are normal and have to be accepted. I learned an important lesson through that particular experience. I had avoided an entire aspect of my nature because of an unwillingness to confront the vulnerability, no, the shame, that is inhered within physical defeat. It came to me in this way, this may not be historically true, but mythically it is: as a boy I could fight, I had no fear. As an adolescent I was not initiated. As I awoke, I was not shown how to live at the new frequency, I had only women to observe and 'role model'. When violence came, as it does to all teenage boys, I was not equipped and the shame killed a part of me, it put it 'underground'. I was too afraid to try and revive it; it was in adolescence of course that I became a drug addict. I did not become willing to go into the underworld until I killed the person I had to become to survive my youth. When I finally went there, in my middle years, through the means of Jiu Jitsu, I needed a mentor, in this case Chris, to hold the space for me.

CHAPTER SIX

MENTOR FIVE:
THE PARK BENCH MERLIN

I am convinced that to become happy and whole we must emulate the systems and structures that human beings had always created before individual and community needs were deluged in the requirements of subjugating structures. The machines. The machines that make machines of us: agriculture, industry, technology.

Between the pillars of Chris and Jimmy in the trident of mentors that manage my current life, crouched in a cave by the shore, or in a burrow in deep woods, or a tree house, anywhere where hermits go, is Bruce. A growling Merlin. If the Gruffalo ate Carl Jung it would then belch the wisdom of Bruce Lloyd. Forty years clean he practises psychotherapy like a psycho therapist. A thought: maybe all this energy is all one, like Brian Cox, or any physicist, would say, 'It all came from one explosion'; 'It was all contained in a pinhead of matter' or whatever precedes matter. Maybe there are patterns within the limitlessness that recur, like the spiral and the circle. Maybe there are subtler forms that appear through nature, through humans as archetypes: the warrior, the lover, the shaman, the wizard. Some people you just know. Bruce is a hermit at the end of a corridor. Meredith is a wise woman in an electronic monastery. Across your life you will see types and archetypes repeating and teaching, some you know by now you must avoid, others you must embrace and ask to teach you. Others, as you grow, are there for you to teach.

Jimmy told me about Bruce. He said, 'This guy Bruce Lloyd, he's good for men who are where you are now.' Let's face it, he means middle age. I don't recall exactly how many times I had to phone but, let me tell you, it was a few. The surly ol' badger was reluctant to answer the call. I left some pretty funny answerphone messages before getting a response. Eventually I found myself in a surprising, kind of corporate, former Wedgwood pottery building in Vauxhall. Not a new building, one of those places that house multiple businesses and a firm will come and sell sandwiches and snacks at lunchtime. You need a card to get through doors and you press a green button to be released as you leave. It's not as space age as I'm making it sound, focus on the humdrummery of the sandwiches, it gives a more accurate picture. Bruce leads you to his office then gives you a corner chair. It's awash with yellow-brown tones as if the light through the window passes first through an old photograph.

As I unpack the wagon of my hoary old background like P. T. Barnum, 'roll up, roll up', and view the freakish past with its acrobatic neuroses and bearded oddities – my psychological history is a well-told story now, it's hard to be authentic when you've peddled your past on stage and in print and I wanted to get Bruce up to speed, to fast forward through the Oedipal lust and rage and get to the new stuff, the reason I was there, in the beige chair . . . But as I encircle the big top on my unicycle, Bruce has a few tricks of his own and propels his chair aggressively in my direction, like a tramp in a nicked wheelchair. I am filling the space between us with words but Bruce freezes them in the air like a sudden November: 'No, Russell. What is it? What. Is. It?'

When I upward swipe my phone, I forget there is nothing there. That the perfect montage of photographs on my feed that seem to be disappearing beyond the border of the screen, isn't actually whooshing upwards, I am looking at code. When I tap on an app and it enlarges and engulfs the whole screen, it's not like a digital balloon has been inflated, it is just code, creating an image that I have no capacity to understand except on the most rudimentary material level. And even as you read these words, these shapes and cyphers on the page, the meaning they inhere in the mind of the reader is a predetermined order, loaded from infancy. There are levels of reality. Some people look at Sanskrit and see pretty patterns, others see a code that refers to the origins of psychic and material energy and the relationship between them. I watch my cats and dogs in the diplomacy and drama, the fight for food and territory, and they do not query my pondering, they do not know the politics of our house or the world beyond. There are levels of reality. All outer phenomena are the expressions of subtler energy, whether that's your relationship with your mother or the way a phone works.

Bruce moves between levels. The shaman must move between worlds, between planes of being. Following the mystical 'why?', interrogating apparent reality, deeper influences are revealed. The ulterior realm from which understood reality is governed.

The upshot of all this is that when you're having therapy with him it's like you're continually invited to examine the green numbers that make up the Matrix more than Neo's sunglasses. He wants to understand the motivating energies and patterns that make up your psyche and diagnose where they are causing pain. Luckily I am the psychological equivalent of a man walking into a doctor's with a boil on his nose; the problems are bleedin' obvious. Addiction is a grotesque exaggeration of the ordinary; everyone likes to escape through pleasure occasionally, an addict uses this mechanism as an emotional bedrock, as the foundation for their entire being. If one cake is nice then eleven cakes will be eleven times as good. If drinking makes me feel less awkward I will drink all the time. Sex is great, let's make it the centre of life. In each of these cases there are accepted biochemical drives to pursue the behaviour that in the addict become exaggerated, obsessive, compulsive, habitual.

An addict in 12 Step recovery will first address the behaviour that is causing the most pain. Often this is substance misuse, which is a relief because the solution is abstinence, which although difficult is at least simple. You have a problem with drink, stop drinking. You have a problem with heroin, stop taking heroin. All of the 'What about weddings?' is just flannel, not drinking at weddings is a small price to pay for freedom from alcohol dependency. Food is more complex and, in my experience, requires particular expertise to address it, but 12 Step recovery will work once the initial grip is loosened – no easy task. What all these outer phenomena have in common is that they are, as I have said, an expression of a subtler pattern – how could they not be? When I met Bruce I was fourteen years into the cycle of uncovering, analysing and discarding addictive behaviours at a, frankly, glacial pace. So I knew the ropes but still had a lot to learn. Here is what I have learned from working with Bruce.

1. We are wounded. A traumatic event has separated us from our 'intended' path.

2. We are programmed. By our family of origin, culture, school. We are conditioned to have a perspective of reality that (if you're in therapy!) is not working.

3. You can change your perspective.

4. This change, salvation, will come from the wound.

We need mentorship because without it we will go round and round the track of our neurosis like Indie 500 racers with a chequered past and no chequered flag. We cannot see the way out ourselves because the instrument of observation is itself the problem.

If we do not employ conscious mental strategies we will continue to use the unconscious ones, installed prior to awareness. It is painful to become awakened because you feel the presence of patterns to which you were previously numb. My strategies often involved creating relationships which prevented my ascension into adulthood, that suspended a kind of innocence or at least facilitated an infantile disengagement from responsibility. I followed strategies, in collusion with others, that prevented adult embodiment. Practically, I outsourced managerial and financial responsibility to others and this left me vulnerable to exploitation but more importantly prevented me from becoming what I needed to become; a father. The first person we parent is ourselves. What kind of parent to ourselves are we? Negligent or diligent? Loving or indifferent? Active or lazy? We have somehow been persuaded that this discourse and vocabulary is in itself 'new age' or 'woo-woo,' which conveniently creates a population that doesn't know how to look after its own interests.

Bruce, the moss-covered rock, watches as I speak, as if he hears the tunes more than the words. In our weekly sessions I report all and any occasions where I have felt the serene thread that now runs through my life dip or spike, usually spike in my case. The lash of fear in my belly, the terror of trying to live a real life, of letting go of false habits, old perspectives, relationships that are inauthentic. I cleared my life out when the steep disillusionment came. When I said I could leave everything in my life behind, it turned out that I was right and that is what happened. Jimmy said: 'If you want to know if the relationships in your life are only there because you pay those people money, see what happens when you take away the money.' I did this, and what happened is that those relationships did not survive.

In the first part of life you strike out. In the second, you dig down. You dig down into yourself. You put the third cable in, the earth cable. In my case, out in the country with my wife and daughters, another attempt at family, but this time, I'm awake.

As I pass into new awareness, the fear increases; fear is a type of awareness. I watch my daughter's awareness grow and I see how the new mental terrain is occupied. She is still too young to conceive of 'under the bed' but I bet that as soon as she conceptualizes it, there will be a monster there. Fear fills new territories of awareness. It is the same with me, I learn of new spaces and I fill them with fear. The contagion of my early dread still hums. I feel the fear and then my mind in anxious conjecture rushes to reason how that fear could become real. Bruce rides shotgun as I travel the badlands, reassures me, he tells me to move forward.

Note the people around you. Do they want you to grow? Or do they want you to stagnate or diminish? Observe them. Who do they want you to be? You may not need to eliminate them from your life, but you will need to renegotiate. As a mentor I know that Bruce has been through the pain. I can see him still from across the room on a bench, on a green, outside a tube station. The wiseman is untethered, his upward gaze made earthbound life a challenge. The commit- ment to the inner voice makes relationships outside hard. If you can manage to not kill yourself, which is not easy, if you can preserve yourself in addiction or delusion until a guide, an opportunity to escape appears, there may be hope for you.

CHAPTER SEVEN

MENTOR SIX: THE APHRODITE OF THE DAMNED

Manya Bartick has been a therapist for a long time. She is glamorous. I mean the hair and the nails. She has mentored me mostly in my romantic relationships, although I initially saw her alone where she was incredibly nourishing and kind to the damaged child I yet carry. It is in couples therapy that her value is most clear. We attended, my girlfriend and I, in an attempt to get along better in a relationship which would not ultimately survive, but perhaps that is an unfair ambition, with lifespans being what they are these days. That said, the relationship only lasted a year and was a pain in the arse for most of it. I'm not blaming the woman I was with; I can be a pretty challenging romantic partner with my blend of limit-less appetites and needs and my instinct to cut off when wounded. I could've been a better friend to this woman but I'd gambled my mental health on her moods, I'd cast her in the role of a deity when she had the limitations of a human. I'd constructed my ideals from the wrong manual, the demented manual of our culture, which instructs us to view our partner as part magical sprite and part Saint John's Ambulance volunteer. My own strain of idiocy always led me to see women as sky-high, rarefied, unobtainable and unreal. Always astonished when anyone was attracted to me I'd go a bit giddy and fall in love too quickly. My mind would race up the aisle to the altar, I'd be covered in confetti midway through the first date. I wanted to save them and I wanted them to save me; it was all so high stakes – love at the point of a loaded gun. I still feel euphoric to recall any occasion where women have found me attractive, like approval is a transfusion of vital blood. This I suspect is common. Maturation deferred, indefinitely if possible, in favour of juvenile oxytocin.

Whilst the relationship didn't work out – or at least didn't endure until one of us died – it was a hugely informative and transformative experience, it exposed a lot of my flaws, my neediness, my co-dependency and the warped manner in which I was unconsciously selecting partners to initiate relationships that could not succeed; simple incompatibility.

Across the coffee table on the low sofas in Pimlico, Manya sits sunken and empathetic. Her primary skill is a deep empathy with women and sympathy for men. Counselling in a relationship still appears to be somewhat taboo, lots of my friends appear averse. Is it because of the presumed sanctity of a marriage? The privacy of a partnership? Are you, like me, a revoltingly uncensored version of yourself in your most intimate partnership? A loose and slovenly blancmange in comparison to the cultivated public persona. This is why counselling is vital for me: I lose my perspective in a relationship. My tendency is to set my partner up as the fulcrum and emissary of all reality, like they are World Secretary, responsible for everything from the whereabouts of my keys, to life after death. Good therapists, who I here submit are different from mentors only in name, have a capacity to feel and intuit the requirements of their client. Whilst therapy can be underwritten by myriad methods and techniques, in practice they are dealing with human beings who are hard to quantify or categorize, especially when it comes to subtle mental patterns and psychic habits. What uniformity is there in depression? There must be such variety according to the peculiarity of the patient. Impossible to take an accurate biopsy of such subjective conditions as lethargy, sadness and despair. So whoever it is on the chair or sofa opposite you needs to be able to feel you in the space between. To deduce what you need from your breathing and your eyes. My faith in Manya's compassion was sufficient to withstand the expiration of the first relationship that she counselled me through. In fact it enhanced my faith in her abilities. She helped me to see that it was a lost cause, that you can never base a relationship on the hope that the other person will some day change. You are in a relationship with the person as they are today. If they want to change themselves that's encouraging but you will never change them.

My wife and I leapt into therapy with ridiculous haste. Our second date was marriage guidance. We'd dated a decade before and had a beautiful time but were not ready for commitment. I in particular was like an unmanned lawnmower chewing through a jungle of possibility. When we found each other again there was a real 'cut to the chase' mentality, like an arranged marriage that we arranged ourselves. 'Do you want children? Where do you want to live?' A blunt acceptance that there is no point in doing this for popcorn and blowjobs. We'd both come out of relationships that were of the demented romance variety and were ready for something different. Manya's recruitment was swift, she provided objectivity and compassion and advocated for patience. She was able to point out where we were defaulting to fear-based attitudes, where we were being incommunicative. Importantly, she encouraged us to assess our unspoken intentions. Sometimes we don't rationally address what we want or what we believe, we carry unconscious templates from inherited sources as diverse and as daft as family and films. 'What do you think a relationship should be like?' 'What do you see your role as in this relationship?' 'What are your responsibilities?' 'What are your expectations?' These questions didn't consciously occur to me in previous relationships, they certainly weren't explicitly addressed. But they always come up. If a month into living with someone you find yourself disgusted by their standard of tidiness it is because these questions were not addressed. If a year into your marriage you are completely bored with your sex life it is the same thing. In the marital ceremony, all the 'richer or poorer', 'sickness and health' stuff is supposed to assert the final nature of your new bond that contains these vacillitating extremes. But the language seems phatic, it might as well be the lyrics to 'Agadoo'. 'Do you promise to push pineapple, shake a tree?' Perhaps the inability of the secularized church to tackle the reality of human relationships is one of the reasons for its ongoing decline.

When we attended a mandatory course in order to use a quaint village church as the set for our wedding the vicar seemed embarrassed by the idea of God. Our rituals have been divorced from the deeper meaning to which they were solely intended to refer. Why do we cry at weddings? What is being evoked? The veils and the marches, the rings and the maids, what do they refer to? Certainly death as well as rebirth is evoked in this ceremony. Are you willing to let go of the man you used to be? Of the plan you used to have?

Where in your life are you encouraged to seriously consider these questions? Are you not astonished that the space for human reflection has been colonized by consumerism and commerce? People are too 'fucking' busy to think about those questions and so relieved are we to have a moment of respite from the pointless drudgery of jobs we just browse Facebook or flick on a screen. I knew my previous formula for selecting mates was not working and was poorly resourced, I was looking for goddesses and projects, not companions and partners. I had odd ideas of what my role would be, more saviour than provider. I felt I could preserve my wayward youthful persona by prioritizing my identity as a performer above all else. All of us have strategies, but the strategies are limited; when you reach the limit you will likely need a mentor to guide you over the threshold. When I realized I wanted to be a husband and a father I knew that I would need some pretty hefty software updates. I did not have a family model to emulate. My mother's family of origin was ruptured by a divorce and the toxic shame still shudders through the survivors like a private Chernobyl. My dad's father died when he was seven, he skidded into fatherhood, mapless.

Mine was a quiet and lonely childhood, in here where I still reside. Whilst I politically and ideologically believe in tribe, family and the collective, I have been raised an individualist; the recipe: doting mother, absent father, no siblings, highly alert, low self-esteem – an off-the-shelf cake mix for narcissists, dictators, kooks and crooks. Drowning in the impossible and the possible, for both are in the infinite, I clung to any floating thing – class clown, show-off, truant, performer, addict – always looking for the light within, without. If you survive your childhood with your spirit intact, if you get through the various disappointing institutions unextinguished at some point, if you're lucky, you may have an encounter with an awakened soul, a kindred spirit. God, it might be a book, or a song on the radio, but for your sake I hope it's a living, breathing mentor, someone who can see your light and has kept their own light burning. As if pulled into a side street in a riot they take you to one side and say 'you have it too', and 'this is the way out'.

One of Manya's strengths in my particular case is that she has now witnessed me as an individual, as a participant in a failing relationship and now as a member of a healthy one. She knows me. She is in recovery herself and knows how addicts think, presumably through scars accrued on her own ordinary odyssey, and knows how they avoid, negate, destroy and explode. She witnesses and translates as my wife and I try to communicate, marshalling my anxious tendency to control and hers to avoid, and directs us to common ground.

Hers is a warm and powerful emotional intelligence, founded on maternal compassion. My rhetorical skills and linguistic gymnastics are easily enveloped and discarded by the potency of her kindness and understanding. As a mentor for the man that must be a father and a husband to daughters and a wife, her strength and intuition are potent. All these people to whom I have turned in making this family are in their own way mad, people with pasts littered with mistakes. I can only guess that they, like me, when invited to fill the role of guide, access an aspect of themselves not only unsul-lied by failure but elevated by it.

———

CHAPTER EIGHT

MENTOR SEVEN: THE DIVINE MOTHER

You know when someone says, 'Come and stay at our ashram in Southern India,' and you say 'I will' whilst simultaneously thinking – 'Yeah, like I'm going to an ashram. I don't even know what an ashram is'? Well, about five years ago, I actually went.

I now know that an ashram is a community that is run on spiritual principles. In this instance Amrita, near Kochi in Kerala, is founded on the philanthropic ideology of Amma; if you know of Amma at all it will be as the Indian woman who tours the world dishing out cuddles to anyone who wants one.

When I first heard of 'the hugging saint' I thought, how can you get to be a saint just by hugging? My understanding was that you have to do at least three miracles that are then verified by the Vatican. I suppose my fervently competitive nature is incensed by the notion of another's canonization – 'That's not fair, I want to be a saint,' I think. Plus, if epic physical interaction is now a milieu that's acknowledged in the mystic realm I'd like to trade in my previous promiscuity for something more spiritually substantial. Like sainthood.

This frivolity aside, I first met Amma in Manhattan years ago with my mate Eddie Stern, who happens to be one of the world's foremost yoga teachers. Interesting how the world of eastern spirituality, a world that defies form and deifies oneness, is still beset by fierce hierarchy. At least it is when it comes into contact with my individualistic conditioning.

This conditioning means I bring cynicism and competitiveness to all new data and, as such, when first introduced to the carnival that surrounds Amma, there was a director's commentary of doubt underscoring the gentle awe of our first meeting. Within the 5,000-seater venue, beyond the Amma calendars and other more bizarre forms of merch, upon the stage she sat, devotees around her conducting the complex midwifery that accompanies each hug. Due to the surge of cuddle-hungry punters an infrastructure has been designed around the ritual that is a bit like a baptism and a bit like the queue for Space Mountain in Disney World Florida. As you near the front, certain that the hours of waiting are at an end, a new, sub queue appears, as you snake towards the giddy ascension.

At the summit, Amma, which is Malayalam for 'Mother', is backed by swamis and sari-swathed acolytes. There is no grandeur, no messianic staring or theatrical laying on of hands, just a dark brown woman dressed in white, giving out cuddles and sweets. In my cultural catalogue, which, let's face it, was printed in Essex, the only reference I could reach for was visiting Father Christmas's grotto in Debenhams, Lakeside.

The first embrace that I received was simple. No fireworks but a distilled maternal warmth, that hummed with infantile comfort. As I knelt and sank into Amma's embrace she murmured something into my ear in a language I didn't understand but seemed to remember.

I thought about the experience a lot. Why has this simple practice conducted by a fisherman's daughter from Southern India become a global phenomenon? What need is being met? What is being issued along with that hug?

The next time I met Amma was in December a couple of years ago at Alexandra Palace. I heard from a delightful hippie lady at a book-signing I was doing that Amma was in town. I went along with my mate Mick and the filmmaker Adam Curtis, who is Tolkienesque in demeanour and gargantuan in intellect. The idea of dragging him off to be cuddled down the Ally Pally, all jammed with seekers and freaks, gave me a real kick.

Like in New York, the vast space was packed with people wanting, on the surface at least, a cuddle. It was while waiting on the stage having had my hug that a bespectacled and youthful swami said to me, 'Come stay at our ashram in Kerala sometime.' 'I will,' I said. 'Fat chance,' I thought.

And yet here I am, on this slender, tropical peninsula that was briefly submerged by the tsunami in 2004 and where Amma was born fifty-odd years ago. We were ferried by Brian

(C'mon, C'mon Let's Stick Together), an American, who met us at the airport and became 'Goatem' as we crossed the threshold of the ashram, like Batman when the signal goes up. He explained that Amma was serving lunch to everyone and if we went straight away we'd be fed. I was knackered and really wanted to go to my room but sensed to do so would be seen as a snub. 'Don't snub a saint,' I thought, worried I might get cursed or bad voodoo so I compliantly shuffled along.

The ashram is like the smugglers bar in *Star Wars*, filled with jostling oddities: backpackers, swamis, locals, yokels, some silent some vocal, Indians, Americans, Brits, Germans, swarming in chaotic harmony. A giant pink temple with stone elephants and garlands is the central point and pink residential tower blocks flank it. It's bigger than I expected and more vibrant. The initial scene of dusty wonder is just for starters though, for rounding the corner to where I'm told Amma is, there is a secondary quad of buildings; a cafe, more homes and a covered aircraft hangar-like structure filled with thousands, literally thousands, of people and at the front sits Amma, children at her feet, devotees all about her, serving up grub. We are taken to the front to see her and get fed and it's bizarre. As I take a plate from Amma, who smiles at me through the mayhem, I turn and thousands of eyes are on me, or rather her, and I'm a temporary obstacle. I do a sort of Kenneth Williams 'oooh' face and get a little laugh from Amma and the crowd.

Like you, I am suspicious of anything that seems too good to be true; like you, I've been trained to judge the actions of others in accordance with my own rather more basic motivations. If you too question the intentions of people who help others then get ready for an epic inquiry. Amma, who many here believe to be a divine incarnation of the Goddess Kali, has done some incredible humanitarian work, including building five universities across India, several hospitals providing free healthcare for the poor, vocational training centres, an orphanage, hospices, 125,000 free homes for the homeless, 50,000 free meals a month for the poor, monthly pensions for destitute women, free clinics, and disaster relief for the tsunami and Hurricane Katrina. Even if you strip Amma's achievements of all spiritual accoutrements, the chanting, hugging and praying, you're still left with a sort of Indian Oprah Winfrey.

For a woman of such humble birth to have contributed so richly would have to constitute at least one miracle, I thought, as I reclined on the hard, flat bed of the basic room on the seventh floor of one of the blocks where I stayed. The Oprah comparison seems less trite as I survey the treats that have been laid on in the room: Amma-branded chocolates and soap; her image adorns posters and products throughout the ashram, and if you cynically query this as I did, then I suppose we need to take a good look at our own western idolatry, which centres on such worthy icons as celebrity chefs and giant transforming robots. Obviously I want to believe that Amma, between hugging the multitudes and feeding the masses, is a decadent fraud who lives in clandestine opulence scoffing down her own chocolates and at her own naive worshippers. When I visit her dwelling for a chat this aspersion is cast aside. She lives in a flat similar to the one I'm staying in – aside from a few accrued religious knick-knacks – yards from the house where she was born.

The ashram has organically sprouted from this site and the initially suspicious villagers, who thought Amma was a nut when she was growing up (she went round hugging everyone), now adore her. The breakthrough came with the ashram's instantaneous and efficient response to the tsunami. Amma herself was wading through the flood setting up relief camps and consoling the bereaved, even before the second wave hit. In many respects Amma could be regarded as a remarkable secular leader; she gets things done. On the subject of the existence of God she said, 'The question is not is there a God but is there suffering?'

Evidently there is suffering and the averred solution is loving pragmatism. Such is the positive impact of Amma's work that if I found out she'd murdered a couple of people on her way to the top I'd think it forgivable, but it seems there are no skeletons in the closet. In fact looking around her flat I can't see a closet – if she had one she'd probably let an orphan sleep in it.

I asked Amma about politics. She answered through her interpreter that the world of politics is so corrupt that it automatically weeds out the well-intentioned, and anyone sincere will be subjected to pestilent mud-slinging. An analysis that's hard to dispute, although I'm never fully relaxed when communicating through a translator. When I interviewed the Dalai Lama a few years ago I'm pretty sure, judging from His Holiness's sour expression, that his interpreter ballsed up a few of my sizzling wisecracks. Misinterpretation was the only possible reason, the jokes were solid.

With Amma I put in a few untranslatable words, like famous names, to circumnavigate the problem. For example, when asking if Amma's spiritual nature is divine, how can it be conveyed or taught? Here I cited the genius of Diego Maradona as an analogy. 'Diego Maradona was a sublime player but not so good as a coach because genius is non-transferable; if Amma is a kind of spiritual genius how can we normal folk learn from her?'

I heard amidst the translator's Malayalam, the native language of Kerala and the only language Amma speaks, the name of Argentina's peerless soccer star, like in a *Fast Show* sketch.

What Amma has intuited, or was born knowing, is that everyone wants to be loved and that everyone is worthy of love. Like a mother she loves unconditionally and serves expediently.

What she demonstrates, we in our loveless social structures are scrabbling to discard. In Amma we have an example of what can be achieved if we build upon the principle of love. Throughout our crumbling culture there is fear, desire and anger, and more and more we all need a hug. Amma's practice may exemplify a simple solution to our spiritual sickness: we can start to change the world by loving each other.

Her answer to the Maradona enquiry pertained to the presence of divine gifts in everyone but I wasn't entirely sure that the question had been understood. I repeated it later to some western devotees while eating. This time, away from Amma's gently shimmering presence, I'm more candid in my syntax: 'In me there is an animal that wants to kill and fuck, how can anyone like Amma, born divinely connected, ever understand that?' Vinay, who first met Amma when he was a boy, thrust into her presence by New Age parents, put it succinctly: 'Perhaps we can never be like Amma, entirely devoted to service and love, but from her we can learn to elevate the aspect of ourselves that is and perhaps as a result, the world as a whole.'

The people I hung out with at the ashram were cool, from the fully switched-on swamis who emanated ochre kindness to the westerners basically like me, lost, lonely and hollow, disillusioned with the religions of the west – materialism, consumerism and individualism – certain that there must be something more.

On New Year's Eve it becomes clearer what that might be. The aircraft hangar is jammed and banging, it's a holy rave-up. Amma has spent the day doing dharshan – that's the cuddles; she goes on for ages, twelve, fourteen, sixteen hours at a time, hugging everyone without discrimination, turning no one away. Then just prior to midnight the kids at the ashram school put on a performance and then Bhajan – a call and response series of songs led by Amma, beautifully accompanied by a dozen musicians on keyboards, bongos and whatnot.

The climactic number is like a football chant germanely dedicated to Kali, the goddess of creation, and at the chorus Amma shouts something and everyone shouts back 'Jai' and I'm sure no one here in this moment feels desperate, hopeless or alone. It's intense. It's like Upton Park. Except obviously at Upton Park desperation was frequently palpable. With each choral holler arms are flung heavenward. The people, together as one.

A leader like Amma is a mentor with more clout, whose impact is a social phenomenon. Clearly then, the most famous members of western culture are mentors of a kind too. We look up to celebrities the way we used to look up to the people around us before we knew celebrities existed. Any hero or mentor, though, carries only the power imbued by the values they represent. Most of our heroes represent beauty and commerce, power for power's sake. The Nelson Mandelas are few and far between. This lack of meaning in the mainstream of course sends the young scurrying to the extremes; the young, motored by deep hormonal purpose, will not settle for the tasteless pap of the mainstream forever, their urgency will send them into the arms of the red-faced and bawling, the flag wavers and the torch carriers, the face painters and the heathens.

CHAPTER NINE

MISSED CHANCES: BEFORE THE STUDENT IS READY

I first realized that Pete was remarkable at a convention for addicts at a hotel in Birmingham where such things are held, that is to say, a mediocre hotel. A convention for addicts has more variety than you might imagine, many classes of people, ages, etc. If there is a common bond it is derived from the shared solution. Ex cons, people with pink hair, a fair few coach trips from treatment centres. A lot of smoking.

I'd met him once before at an event at a treatment centre in Birmingham where I'd said a few words and he'd sung a few songs. Since then he appeared to have acquired crutches and he swung enthusiastically through the crowded lobby to say hello. I suppose the presumed temporary nature of crutches makes it okay to ask what the injury was in a way sensibly forbidden by wheelchairs or even canes, the general rule being 'crutches, funny story, cane, sad story'. I asked Pete what had happened and he, and this is odd, smilingly responds, 'I have cancer and I'm having my leg amputated.' The news is unusual but it's the smile that's most strange. I, aghast, say, 'Oh, fuck, I'm sorry.' And he says, 'No, I'm okay, I'm clean and I want to live.' Now when he says this it is entirely without bravado and with the kind of certainty that, if I'm honest, I've never seen in anyone other than the spiritually switched on. By definition in fact, Pete's connec- tion to a Higher Purpose was so strong that his forthcoming amputation was irrelevant. I'm very good at saying 'the material world is an illusion', I'm less good at blithely brushing off cancer as if it is the will of the universe. I was in awe at Pete and started to keep in contact with him, in a way to study him, curious as to whether he was for real, to see if at some point he would yield to self-pity or rage. He didn't. He FaceTimed me from his hospital bed and showed me the bandaged stump before the anaesthetic had worn off. I was at a charity car wash which I'd impulsively been drawn to by the attire of the women conducting it, but such baser motiva-tions were washed away on talking to this saintly man, joking from his post-operative bed.

I'm mates with another bloke who's had a leg ampu-tated, Will, who is like Balloo from the *Jungle Book*, a big cuddly, handsome, hulking thug. The first time I met him I knew I'd like him, he was loud and aggressive and vulner-able. He works with the street homeless in Oxford and he announced himself to me and the group of men we were hanging out with by recounting the tale of his journey to our group meeting, in which he'd got out of his car to have a row with a fella who had cut him up on the M40, a key detail being the reattachment of his leg prior to getting out of the car and punching the bloke. This was told with a kind of breathless, post-adrenaline regret, not mournful, but with a 'whoops, I let myself down there' Englishness that was very endearing. When I met Pete I thought I should connect them. Pete was about to go through a procedure that Will had already experienced and it seemed like an obvious connection to make.

The two men chatted and by all accounts got along and I was able to modestly contribute to Pete's recovery – to be honest though, given his incredible aptitude for positivity, he'd've been fine anyway. When we last spoke he told me, again without bitterness, or even sadness, that the cancer had likely spread to his lungs and he faces another proce-dure. I hold Pete in my mind as an antidote to self-pity. Perhaps if we spend time around positive people, being posi-tive to one another, we can raise our common frequency as well as our individual wellbeing.

Your own strategy, your native program, will get you so far. Mine got me to the Hackney Empire New Act of the Year Final. I was drunk, I was high, I was a trembling time bomb but I was there. I lived in yet another Lost Boys, Fight Club flat. I signed on, and I slept on a futon with my mate Karl overlooking some public toilets in Bermondsey, South London. I had mates, peers, but not mentors. I'd gotten myself thrown into, then thrown out of a drama school – ironically for being too dramatic – and there were potential mentors there. Christopher Fettes, the Principal of Drama Centre, was part Caesar part serial killer, aloof, grand, magnificent; I, like all the students, adored him. He was a brilliant teacher and arriving as I did at nineteen, essentially a boyband member without a cap, it was Christopher who inundated me with classical references, Nietzsche, semiotics, archetypes; he was a calm cyclone of incredible wisdom. He also made me feel I was great.

I hear addicts like me speak and I know how common it is to crave adulation. Men, who if you saw them eyeing you in a boozer would make you grip your glass a little tighter and steel yourself for kick-off, gently describing the tender need for love. When I was nineteen I wanted to feel love. I was rootless and was trying to suck nutrition out of the air, usually through a pipe. In the environment of that drama school I learned that what I'd always quietly, fiercely believed was true: that the strangeness, the oddness, the 'not quite fitting in' could be a gift, not a latent disability. Somehow though, whether it was through my inability to receive it or the fact that it was not there to receive, I didn't feel nurtured. I felt feted and occasionally great, like I had a dangerous power that might kill me or make me a star, but that wasn't what I needed. I needed to be held.

Eventually I spilled out of that place in a characteristic manner, eliciting the kind of 'sorry, but no' regretful goodbye that addicts become accustomed to. There was a lawless and carousing quality to my behaviour that needed direction, not quite prison or the army but some version of that with more love and more room for creativity and perhaps better food and nicer uniforms.

I think of the men a few generations older than me, conscripted, and remember that they weren't all hard-handed uncles; Kenneth Williams had to do a turn, Spike Milligan, fragile, volatile, strange men, how the hell did they do it? In both of those cases, under duress and ending in misery. When I visit prisons I note the men that are like me, the ones that seem like soft outsiders, that I can't wrangle into my preconceptions of knuckly blokes that look bred for it. Drugs were my mentor and my muse, my miserable belief and my hopeless religion. And they got me as far as the Hackney Empire New Act of the Year Final. I walked the track like an F1 driver the day before the show and was terri-fied by the vastness and the possibility of success. I gave the evening over to drink and drugs, threw all hope at the altar of escape. I was off my head when I went on that stage, that massive stage. I came nowhere near winning but it was enough for me to level-up.

The Empire invited me back to be in a political fund-raiser show – was it the dockers, what was it? Rob Newman was there and it was all too much for me to take. You see Rob Newman had been part of a ludicrously cool and glamorous double act with David Baddiel, maybe ten years earlier, and whilst he had since clearly gone through a number of personal metamorphoses – primarily, plainly, a rejection of that glamour, fame, all that – to me, it was as if there were an archangel in the room. His comedy had always been intellectual, melancholy, erratic, bipolar, great comic voices, suddenly and surprisingly political, and he was dreamily handsome, long haired. I idolized and emulated him before I had any idea that was what I was doing. For him to suddenly be on the same carpet as me was ridiculous. Albeit, this was a grungier incarnation: the hair was shorn, and he had in retrospect violently abdicated the 'rock 'n' roll' aspect of his former celebrity, but that is of course a pretty rock 'n' roll thing to do. Man, I stared before I sidled. I looked at him and drank him in and had no idea how to be normal. I would've given away my ragged soul for a Cyrano to handle the conversation. Instead I went over to the famously shy comedian and coughed up mental illness at him. In all actuality I was roaming around quite drunkenly, a devotee without a faith, a disciple without a guru, a young and mentorless man, reaching out into a world that scared me, ashamed even of my need for guidance.

CHAPTER TEN

———

MENTOR EIGHT: THE BROTHER SWAMI

I was twenty-seven before I met a holy man. I was a default atheist in spite of my inability to gel with the world, its inhabitants and institutions. I didn't consider that I needed a solution beyond materialism, I just thought I needed more material. I was highly suspicious of Jesus; I was introduced to him in the usual C of E way, blank and unconvincing tinsel-spattered dioramas. Hopelessly literal interpretations of the Gospels. Herod, mangers, shepherds, Joseph, angels, wine, fishermen. What am I supposed to do with that in Grays, Essex? Me and my mum were up in London one day – I was ten years old, I feel like I was off school for some reason and it was the hinterland between primary school and high school. I was due to be sent to boarding school and was disturbed by the prospect. Some Mormon evangelists buttonholed us at Baker Street with an invite to look around their educational centre. For some reason I was keen to go. I faintly recall being led round an exhibition outlining Joseph Smith's unlikely discovery and what it meant for us now. I feel like even then the particulars of Mormonism's origin myth struck me as troubling – the missing Gold Plates, Jesus living in America – but I liked the aspiration and I certainly wasn't beneath using the experience to challenge my mum's decision to send me to kiddie-prison. The most vividly recalled moment being when I asked the most vocal Mormon whether he agreed, in theory, with children being sent away to school and him solemnly saying that he did not. Why I thought the views of a passing Mormon would sway my destiny I do not remember, suffice to say I ended up at that school and the rupture was never undone.

Perhaps I was destined to be the type of child who lives inside his head, the teenager that disappears into substance misuse, an adult that craves approval before eventually finding faith and connection; even in my forties it feels like it was pivotal in my severance and mistrust.

I am twenty-seven and just clean and kind of insane. The people around me were bigging up this holy man before I met him. At Bhaktivedanta Manor the devotees were buzzing, the anticipatory air of excitement that precedes the arrival of any high-status individual. The Hare Krsna movement from its arrival in the west has been associated with counter culture and the high-profile inhabitants of that shabbily sparkling realm. Prabhupada, the swami who brought Krsna consciousness to New York and San Francisco, before settling in Watford, of all places, both rode and enhanced the wave of hippie fervour that signalled the end of post-war conformity and the onset of the individualism that began in the late sixties. While awaiting the arrival of his student and heir, Radhanath Swami, I am absent-mindedly drinking in this myth. I am most enamoured of and fascinated by the connection between The Beatles and these be-robed holy folk, the connection between psychedelics and meditation, the connection between the rejection of the material world and the embrace of mysticism. To me, even as a young and uneducated man, there is something important contained within these relationships. We are outdoors, there are an assortment of ordinary British Asians, people in religious capes and blankets with clay on their foreheads, flowers, incense, some cows – all in the grounds of a mansion donated by George Harrison. It is very stimulating. I meet some of the former Beatle's friends – Shamusanda, a puckish Ken Kesey refugee from the sixties, and several other talkative and friendly devotees – before I am directed to Radhanath Swami, who has ghosted in as if on wheels concealed by dry ice and now stands warm, aloof, benign and disruptively silent in a way that I now know is commensurate with enlightenment. I knew there was something appealing about this radiance, something that I needed to understand. Charisma is by its nature appealing in a way that is hard to quantify; it was clear to me this smiling and daunting monk had a connection to something that I needed.

My bespoke pantheon of mentors will unlikely fulfil all of your needs; on the surface you probably have very different requirements to me – you might want to become a florist or a cage fighter and have little need for an assembly of counsellors, TV producers, monks and junkies – but you will need external coordinates of some kind upon which to focus your intention in order to bring into being your latent power. In my forties I can see the strata through which I have passed in order to progress from drug addict, to bewildered performer, to co-dependent love addict. I can see how significant relationships with elders and teachers enabled me to exceed limitations that I was bound by in solitude. I can now speculate more accurately as to what the next levels of progress might be. I know I need to continually learn how to be a better father and husband; I want to learn how to be effective in bringing positive change into the lives of vulnerable people; I want to serve as a conduit for impersonal, powerful forces that have guided human destiny for as long as there have been humans (is that too much to ask!).

These varied intentions will all require that I have a connection to inner power that cannot be accessed through purely rational means. I need to have a relationship with the 'unknowable'. This impulse that led me to bother dear Rob Newman in a green room as I mistakenly believed he had some voodoo he could convey is now better directed at people who understand the nature of my intention and the parameters within which our relationship can operate. Throughout school, drama school, life on benefits and hopeful destitution I was looking for a way out, I was waiting for someone to whisper me the codes. Meanwhile I dealt with the steep city and its low gutters by burrowing through the underworld, alone and intoxicated, unable to receive teaching, even if it were offered.

Radhanath Swami is part of the guru–disciple tradition. He is himself from a western background and spent his early life disenchanted with the solutions that modernity offers to spiritual yearning. Somehow, without conventional instruction, he found his way to India and searched for a teacher who could help him to direct this nameless yearning, this yearning which I now believe is in us all and in its splintered and refracted form accounts for all superfluous desire. He met Prabhupada, for whom he felt immediate love and trust. When I imagine this love that disciples describe feeling when they first encounter their gurus, this love at first sight that Radhanath Swami felt for Prabhupada, that Yogananda felt for Yukteswar that Sheela felt for the Bhagwan, I can only compare it to romantic love. The plunging, elated, deracinating nausea that I have felt a dozen times across my life that surely through some divine lens could yet be viewed as glistening scars across my past. Always a woman, usually a stranger, always temporary, unsustainable. Searing, overwhelming, transcendent love: Anna Dear at eleven, Nikki in the next street at fourteen, Louise at sixteen, Penny, Chloe, Kerry, Amanda, Katy . . . when I view them as a list it becomes almost impersonal, as if they were a living ceremony, a sign that stirred this dormant and demented longing. As I got older I had relationships with these women and fell apart as they descended from the heavens where I'd placed them and to the earth where they belonged. Some of them loved me back. Curiously the feeling in me was no more sophisticated when I was a man than when I was a child. How could this feeling survive the demands of the material world? Of sex and gas bills? How could it endure the mundanity of bad plumbing, burnt toast and erectile dysfunction? This pure and blazing energy that means to pull you home to God and yet seemingly alights on angels. I envy the naturally religious; not nutters, not homophobes or those fixated on controlling others – that's not religion. I mean those who quickly see that no material thing will ever make them feel whole, but that the invisible world is humming with love and they are able to connect to it. I fantasize about donning some 'religious garb', a robe, a dog-collar, a habit, even, and perhaps especially a blanket, to denote my resignation from formal society and my member-ship of the mystical. If only I'd known at eleven that I would never satiate the bilious compulsion through romantic obses-sion, that only a Higher Purpose would do – ah, the savings on chocolates, flowers and gold-plated bracelets, the poems and the inconvenience to uninterested women.

It has been said: 'Addicts are not enslaved by drugs, drugs serve as an escape from the false ideals of a materialistic society.' Our ideals are false. Our patriotism, our religion, our consumerism, our romanticism, our individualism – all false ideals of a materialistic society. Ideals that are used to ensure that material resources remain in the control of a limited group. Myths and stories, philosophies and systems congeal around this simple truth. What is it that is trying to express itself through the yearning I felt for those girls and women? I can tell you candidly it was not lust. They were almost always asexual quests I had unconsciously nominated these females as symbols of divinity, holiness, wholeness, completion, because I felt incomplete, tarnished, dirty.

Infidels, without fidelity, out of alignment with the 'true frequency'. Like a needle that cannot ride the record's groove. What is the 'true frequency'? Are we really living in a post-truth world? Or does even that claim belie our awareness that there is an absolute truth that we are now failing to acknowledge? What are the values to which we refer? Forget God, what is good? What is kindness? What is love? And those who claim these too to be constructs are they not just wounded cynics, hurt and without hope? There is no measure of space or molecule sufficient to eliminate love. There is no way to step outside of the sphere of our sensory realm and its obvious limits to declare, 'There is nothing out there, there is nothing in here.' Those that would deny the sublime on the basis of the gross are making a leap of faith greater than any believer, they are excluding the possibility that there are phenomena that exceed our understanding, and the short history of our tiny kind has shown again and again that the limits of our knowledge are not the limits of knowledge itself. Neither do we possess the instruments to assess what true knowledge may entail. Therefore Faith. Therefore Acceptance. Therefore Love.

And yet we live as infidels, faithless, out of the groove of the invisible sublime, scratching through life as if we were just bodies, mouths, stomachs and shit and cum. This is the world materialism begets, this is the legacy of rationalism, strip away the iPhones and the comfort and this is our contract; we trade connection for distraction.

It is popular to reiterate, largely because of the irrefutable persuasiveness of Dr Jordan Peterson, that with values come hierarchies, that our order is immovable. But if we cherish the methods that enable us to inwardly connect, then we experience the depth of our sameness and the superficiality of our difference and we realize that outward systems that give precedence to our difference, even when underwritten by apparent values, are disingenuous, in that they contradict the deeper truth of our connection.

In order to live like this as an individual, let alone as a culture, we need mentors that have managed to overcome the systems that we are born into. For me as a white, western, working-class male, now economically privileged, I need mentors that know every aspect of that journey; not every mentor needs to know every aspect, but I do need guidance in each area. It's not that my sole goal is to smash the state and dismantle the machinery of capitalism, I've done very well out of the state and capitalism. I'm typing this in a lovely house on a nice computer, I'm aware of how much worse it could be because it has been much worse for me, personally. Also, I do not doubt the horrifying tales I hear of suffering in Bangladesh as they struggle to accommodate Burmese refugees, or of the embattled people of Palestine, or even of the homeless of High Wycombe, but fifteen minutes away. I know I am lucky, materially and in many other ways. But the same way I can trace my adolescent infatuations to ill-fated marriage and ultimately to spiritual connection, I can trace my sense of personal injustice and longing for fairness to a broader more general belief that the world must become more fair. We all feel it, and the feeling is not naivety, it is the intuitive knowledge that a better reality is trying to be born through us.

The mentors I need now are to help me to maintain my connection to duty as a husband and a father, my focus as a professional and a provider, but I also need mentors to help me navigate the void within me to the planes where continuing external change is possible. I need men and women that have rejected the systems that contain me, inner and outer – whether those systems are personal insecurity or consumerism, our programming and conditioning depend upon the relationship between the inner and outer states. Radhanath Swami, like Amma, has entirely rejected the possibility that the material world can bring satisfaction. He prioritizes eternal principles such as compassion and integrity over temporary phenomena like prestige and haircuts. I need to study this as I still have a foot in each camp. Sometimes in meditation I experience impersonal consciousness that I can only recognize in retrospect (because when I am in it there is no I) and I feel the truth in it. Then I feel at some point in the same day lonely or tired, and the first idea that occurs to me is to look at porn or eat cake. 'How do you not succumb to base emotions?' I asked him. He said: 'When I feel jealous or prideful it reminds me that I need to move closer to God.'

Actually it was Karl, my mate, who asked him, on a pleasant and peculiar occasion when the Swami visited our family home, on a day when my mum and her friends Jan and Derek were also present. It was a particular joy to see Jan and Derek, lovely people, perched with tea cups near the silent and beaming Swami. The word 'swami' means 'he who is with himself' and he was certainly with himself then. Everyone else just sat all awkward while he gazed at unfolding scenes from the Bhagavad Gita in the battlefield of his mind. It's also what it's like to be around Morrissey. Everyone else just has to deal with it.

The point is, even elevated souls are subject to the emotions that cause us agitation but they are able to use them as spurs to move closer to the light, more kindling to burn in ascension, rather than ignition for penurious action.

I'm, at point of writing, not planning to become a celi- bate monk, and most orders I've raised the possibility with have made it pretty clear they won't have me. These gurus, though, will continue to mentor me as I relinquish a life where prestige, privilege and power continue to be my objec- tives, deliberately or otherwise. I live in a liminal space, half looking back to the man I used to be, mostly fixed forward on what I am becoming. I often feel the pull as real and as peculiar as gravity, a backward yearning, particularly when all before me is new and – in truth – often unclear.

CHAPTER ELEVEN

FATHERHOOD: HOW TO PRACTISE

The abrupt sudden oxytocin-soaked slap in the face of parenthood has sent me reeling and the whole point of parenthood is to be stable. I am the father of two little girls and my job is to be a nurturing protective constant while these two females pass through hormonal tundras and emotional hurricanes. Parent. Parenthesis. Again, to hold them, like this ( ) while they grow. Unfortunately a man with my unreasonable degree of sensitivity, my tendency to smell the lurking sacred, sees threats to their sanctity everywhere. Our first social engagement with our first daughter was another kid's party, and people come looming and cooing at the baby I am holding, and I want to quickly puncture their tracheas with a fast darting spearing blow to the neck. I bargain myself down to slapping away the never ending flock of (as far as I know) unwashed hands and this alone creates tension. I see her as being just like me and I wouldn't want, I don't want, people I don't know coming over and touching my head. This coupled with my willingness to kill, which seems somehow like a newly relevant duty, not an abstract possibility, meant that the kid's party had a little more aggres-sion than was necessary, much of it emanating from me.

Neither do I like tickling. Before I was a father I was a right pain in the arse, Johnny come lately interloper at a party, razzing up kids with daft voices, sugar and excitement; tickling was a de rigueur part of my game. I had this thing I'd do called 'The Driller Killer' where I'd wheedle the shank of the hysterical child with my finger, held, as the name suggests, like a drill. A regular victim of this was Ezra Baddiel, my friend's son, and I must say, Your Honour, he loved it. He laughed and we chased each other and capered and screamed and had a bloody good relationship that went way beyond the tickling and into chats, play and, I hope, good counsel. But even to recall doing this to Ez fills me with dreadful shame and makes me want to punch myself in the face. Which is what I will do to anyone who tickles either of my daughters until they are old enough to decide for themselves whether they want to be tickled or not, which by my reckoning is at thirty-five. I loathe it, it is an attempt to subvert the child's bodily autonomy, to take control of them, to take away their right to their own space and peace. Would you do it to an adult? Would you approach an adult and insert your rigid fingers into their belly or their armpits? Of course not. I've actually enraged myself by thinking about it – reformed ticklers, like ex-smokers are always annoyingly evangelical. What, though, when the transgressor against your child is a child themselves? What then? Not with tickling but with any kind of disrespectful, less than doting and reverent behaviour?

We have friends with children, of course we do, that's life now. It seems but the twinkling of an eye ago that my life was all Lear Jets and enthusiastic orgies, well now it's play-dates and there is nothing playful about a playdate. It's an unrestrained, unmanaged, dangerous experiment that places my precious, perfect little girl in the company of anonymous, unvetted, potential arseholes.

Our lovely friends came round with their two-year-old when my daughter was about ten months old. These are good people. Kind, generous, fun, warmhearted, wise, lovely people. They come round, flowers, food, good-quality gifts, and let their child roam freely into our kitchen. My daughter was just walking at that point and was excited, visibly, at this new social possibility. She is barely yet formed, she is mostly pure light and golden hair. The memories that stretch back to her conception are so few, new and cherished that I can hold the whole of her being in my mind, moment to moment as I watch the cells in her immaculate face divide and grow. This boy walked up to her, my daughter, this living and breathing irrefutable proof of God's love, and pushed her in the face with the bolt-armed, right-angled palm of a Rugby League scrum half. It was like someone had fired a gun. An involuntary yelp was cut from deep within me that filled the silence between the push/punch/strike (maybe we need a new word for this? Prunk?) and her tears. Now of course I know this is normal kid behaviour. Life. But that was the first time it had happened. That was the first time anyone had been anything other than loving to her in her whole life. My hope was that I would be able to chaperone her through life, from inception to expiration without even an ill breeze disturbing her perfection. To stretch the womb to the tomb, a life in utero where she is constantly enshrined and protected and nourished, never truly born to the world until the grave. My infallibility cracked like Nimrud antiquities under Islamic State attack.

It took a while to get my breath back. I told Chris at the next BJJ session. I suppose I do BJJ because I want to protect my family. I said: 'What do you do about all this, the tickling? The other kids? The touching at parties?' He said: 'You just gotta suck that stuff up.' Pretty simple. But my fear, I suppose, is that I am inadequate and incapable of protecting my family specifically because I'm not a badass BJJ blackbelt; Chris is and it makes no difference. This is life and it's okay to be you, it's okay to be me. Jimmy said, 'They move further and further away from you; first they are in your arms, then they toddle at your feet, then school, university, work, until . . .'

I anxiously awaited the outcome of the twelve-week scan and I said to Meredith, 'Once you get through the twelve-week scan, 90 per cent of pregnancies succeed. If we can just get through the twelve-week scan . . .' She said, 'Yeah. Then it's the twenty-week scan, then the twenty-eight-week scan, then the thirty-six-week scan, then the birth, then playschool, then school, then the wedding. You're a hostage to fortune now, for the rest of your life.'

———

This spiritual life, in the end it is not a choice, it's what's left when you run out of choices. If when you're in a crowded room you automatically find yourself thinking 'all of us in this room will die. Someone will be the first to die, and someone the last to die, but there is an order,' then gloomily ponder what the order might be, I suggest that you are already excluded from material solutions to the spiritual problem of being alive.

All of us live suspended on a canyon wire between the person we used to be, the person we are ascending and the person we are aspiring to become. Every day the pugilistic slog goes on for me. A snidy little text, a curt comment, a holy soft focus act of benevolence to a slumped stranger. I'm back and forth between the kind and ideal me, sometimes self-consciously, and the 'Venom' version of myself, all fangs and inner eelish sinew, writhing. Sometimes I appear in films, unable to entirely give myself up to the caves and blankets – I mean, I have daughters and being in a film, if undertaken quite gently, I've discovered can be a pleasant experience. Now though the days of mirrored shades and entourages are gone. Now I find myself driving to Ireland, where the filming of *Four Kids And It* will take place, in a Land Rover heaving with kids and dogs; we have a roof rack for fuck's sake, a roof rack. A ferry is involved and stops to walk dogs and feed infants, mobile domesticity, a travelling family. From beneath the nappies and dog hair and that stink that dogs in cars brew with such abundance, as if fearing a forthcoming stink famine, I think, 'Wow, the MTV VMAs'; 'Wow, the premieres, the police escorts and jets', the eerie privilege, the rootless gaseous glory of fame, gone. Of course, I'm driving to the location of a film that will have Michael Caine in it and Cheryl Cole, not a bareknuckle boxing match in Limerick but still I'm in a different world. I do not deplore the time of cellophane celebrity, I'm kind of in awe of it; hosting *Saturday Night Live*, the cover of *Rolling Stone*, shirtless – 'Who was that man?' And in all honesty did I leave the party early, despairing at the emptiness, or was I asked to leave because I failed to reach invisible box office targets? The latter, the latter to the letter. But now I think, 'God has greater plans for you than mere movie stardom.' Here in the fug of Alsatians and retrievers, inhaling wet clouds of dog breath, I think, 'Thank God *Arthur* didn't make $100 million' – or I'd still be in the luminous morgue begging corpses for redemption.

In the chapel of Brixton prison I sat breathing only in the top inch of my lungs. Thick with nerves about the unfolding event: 'Letters Live', where letters of note are read by people with profiles. The empty adjacent chair awaits Benedict Cumberbatch. We all await Benedict Cumberbatch, that's the law; the most famous person arrives last and I think about this as I wait, imprisoned. The tablet on the wall that confronts me, intended of course for the convicted, informs us in lapidary the verse from Isaiah: 'Fear not, for I have redeemed you, I have called you by your name, you are mine.' Redeemed need not be saved or forgiven, redeemed here means regain; you no longer belong to yourself so your fear is redundant, irrelevant, pointless. You belong to God, you belong to death, the death to which you fall like a stone, a stone in water, slowed but falling, gawping at passing experience, at times so enveloping that it's easy to forget that we are falling at all, easy to forget that we are owned, owned by death, owned by God.

We arrive in County Wicklow, my wife, my babies and I, and I try to settle into the role. I try to see what it is I'm meant to be doing, it's so unfamiliar, you see. To be a father and a husband on a work trip to County Wicklow in a lovely rented house, a bit too near to the motorway for my liking. I mean I know how to handle a problem like that as a movie star: you tantrum the fuck out of that too-near motorway until all in screaming distance are bowed and bend what used to be their will but is now yours to ensuring either you, the house or the motorway are moved. But the T&Cs are different as a dad, and if you don't know that, you don't know much.

The film and the house are all easy, the walks with the dogs in the fields behind the house are all easy. In fact most of life is easy except the cracking and refracting madness diagonalling through my mind in cruel unending triangles. 'Ooh, I see the *Mamma Mia* Immersive Dining Experience is coming to the O2,' says my wife. And I see where this is going and more importantly where I am not going. I am not going to the *Mamma Mia* Immersive Dining Experience at the O2, not because I don't like Abba or *Mamma Mia* or Immersive Dining Experiences or even the O2, especially, but because I know that were I to attend the *Mamma Mia* Immersive Dining Experience at the O2 I would not be immersed. I would be in my own head questioning and answering the experience; I wouldn't be able to lose myself there, I would actually find myself more severely than ever. I would be intensely me like a flashing blue light of me. Like a tangerine strobe on a fast dual carriageway. Me with sirens, me with foil blankets, urgent emergency me; *me-naw*, *me-naw*, *me-naw*. I can't lose my self in fucking Greek waiters, 'Waterloo' and ersatz menopausal ecstasy, me won't go limp for that, me will be covered with a thousand lidless eyes, every surface an eye, eyes like scales, eyes dragging across the concrete floor of the O2, eyes full of disco and pastiche, smashed plates and checked tablecloths, eyes unable to stop seeing. Eyes craving the brown silence of heroin, or the blind gurgling bliss that trails orgasm with a stranger. 'My, my; how could I resist you?'

Suspended on a sprawling web of newly formed synapses, spun by arachnoid love, I need to be held myself. I need mentors that can bear the tension of these fast expanding, high vibrating threads so the father can be woven and hold it all together. Christ.

CHAPTER TWELVE

BECOMING A MENTOR

I asked, tentatively, some of the lads I mentor if there was anything they'd learned from our relationship that I could write about. I told them about this book. I told them that mostly this book is about my mentors but that mentorship is a line, a thread upon which we are hung, and it runs through us and beyond us and that there is some comfort in that. There's a trio of lads I work with in London, who I know through support groups for people with addiction. They all work in the city in various capacities but are more from the barra' boy, chancer gang than the pinstriped variety. They are all mates. I'm not using their real names, for reasons that will become obvious.

The first one that I began to mentor, let's call him Max, was someone I'd liked a good while before we connected. A soulful and solid, doe-eyed individual with the bolshie pluck you need to survive in EC1 and young offenders institutions. He'd been clean a while then relapsed, primarily due to his unbelievably unhealthy and insane co-dependent relationship. Listening to him describe the circumstances of his relapse was laugh-out-loud crazy and involved crack and violence, and I could almost hear the screeching of tyres and sirens as he spoke. Characteristically for an addict, the lashing insanity of the story was greatly at odds with the sweetness of the person reciting it. I told him if he wanted help, I was happy to help him. We started to work together, mostly we focused on the nature of his co-dependent relationship and how it would, unless radically altered, ultimately lead to drug use and other unhealthy behaviour. We noted how without the distraction of a co-dependent partner other problematic behaviours escalated. This we did using the 4 column method common to 12 Step abstinence programs. This technique helps you to identify patterns in your behaviour and the emotional and psychological problems that underwrite them. Once the patterns and problems are identified, it is easier to elect to use different strategies to deal with life. Much of this centres on the surrender of self will, letting go of what you think is right, and becoming teachable.

Through Max I met his mate Stan, a giant, charismatic and adorable man who I instinctively liken to Omar, one of the four Caliphs to succeed The Prophet. A bountiful and warm soul with a great strength, yet to be refined. I asked Stan: 'Is there any way I have helped you that I might be able to use in a book about mentoring to illustrate how the principles work?' He said: 'Mate. The other day when that bloke knocked me for that money, you said that I should not look at the people of the world as resources there to serve me but at myself as someone who can help others. To accept that everything won't go my way all the time and when I am disappointed to talk through those feelings before acting on them. In a situation like that in the past I would've acted differently, aggressively, and tried to solve the problem through intimidation, which would've led to complications because this bloke is part of that world. Instead I went round there and politely explained my side of the situation and offered to help find a mutually beneficial solution. This is because you have taught me that I am valuable and I do not need to resort to bad behaviour to get what I want, that I am enough and do not need money to prove that I am a man. I no longer unthinkingly get into conflict with my wife because I am stressed about work-related things, without recognizing it. The other day she asked me to do the washing up because I'd agreed to and I just did it. In the past there would've been an argument, especially if I was fearful around work. This is because you have shown me how to behave towards my wife and given me safe outlets for my feelings.' Hearing this made me feel valuable and useful. The gratitude of others, is a good way to build self-esteem. If you regularly help others the tendency to think of yourself as worthless or not good enough diminishes.

The third of this little triptych is Marco, a flash and blushingly handsome lad who experienced a lot of loss in his childhood and is trying to compensate through excess as a young adult. His sex addiction was a gift to me because he is where I was ten years ago. Sex addiction, if your tastes are socially sanctioned, can take a long time to address. It takes a long time to admit that it is a problem when much of the behaviour is lauded and lionized. When addressing it we have to identify whether it is causing suffering to any party involved. Whether it requires dishonesty or is selfish. In talking to a younger man about sex addiction I get to reaffirm the distance I've been granted from that life and am able to recall the pain that accompanied it, rather than nostalgically yearning for a life that was unhealthy because my memories are biased and my addictive tendency wants me to return to destructive patterns. Marco told me that our relationship had helped him to view his behaviour differently and had awoken in him the possibility of a different life focused on artistic, as opposed to carnal, creativity. He said he feels accepted as who he is and never feels judged or condemned and always comes off the phone feeling better about himself.

In their accounts I see how mentorship is a bilateral arrangement that creates space for a difficult to define third component. In relating to them I am able to register my own progress, because I no longer see the world in the way I used to, when I reach back into my past in order to connect to them, I see how different I have become. Their gratitude heals me. The counsel I offer them, coming as it does down the line from my own mentors and from methods that are proven, is obviously still required in my life, so when I hear myself cite it I think, 'You need to do that yourself, Russell.'

There is nothing negative about being a mentor. Even the fact that it requires me to give my time to others is hugely positive for a person like me whose tendency unguided can be towards the selfish and self-obsessed. If I can be the figure I am in the lives of these young men, then I am better set to be a good husband to my wife and a good father to my daughters. It is the remedy to having lived a life where I'd only hear my own voice whining or screaming, now I hear it calmly offering solutions to sometimes very difficult problems. I am no longer the person I used to be. I am in a state of becoming, guided by principles that are timeless and beautiful, not by the truculent grunts of my endlessly hungry guts or the bloodshot roaming of my greedy eyes. Intention and attention, they say. Where your attention goes, so shall you become. As you intend to be, so shall you be. These relationships, built on selfless love, freely giving what was freely given to me, become a ritual of self-actualization that I would not be granted anywhere in a world built around superficial success and fragile and transient transactions.

The mentor remains conscious when we elide into the old realms, blinded by the old motivations. My podcast is a sanctuary for me and a symposium. Many great educators have joined me, Naomi Klein, Kehinde Andrews, Adam Curtis, Brad Evans, Yanis Varaofakis. Stirred and captivated by the rise of right-wing populism I began to think I'd like to talk to prominent figures from that movement on my podcast. I enquired, made contact and went as far as making an appointment to record an interview with one high-profile activist. The truth behind my motivation is complex, because I am often fuelled by multiple intentions. I do believe that a dialogue between people with different perspectives is vital if we are to change the world. I also feel that the global rise of populism is a legitimate reaction to the failure of the political class to represent the interests of ordinary people. Much of the right-wing rhetoric now is centred on the failure of Neo-liberal politicians to take the financial industry to task and their complicity in the bail-outs. The cost of these actions was borne by ordinary people. Of course, I don't agree with the marginalisation or condemnation of any ethnic or social group as a response to austerity but I am so intrigued to learn if a populist alliance could ever reconfigure democracy that I wanted to focus on the similarities, not the differences.

In addition though to this genuine curiosity, slinking unseen in the shadows of my mind is my ongoing tendency to create chaos, disruption and destruction in my life. I began to feel anxious about it and having consulted a few philosophers and film makers about the way I should approach the interview, I mentioned my anxiety to my wife. She asked if I had spoken to Jimmy or Meredith about it, which I hadn't. When I did, by text, both promptly sent almost identical responses: do not do it, you will create unnecessary tension and conflict in your life. This may not be earth-shattering for you, but for me it is. I actually did what they suggested, I indefinitely delayed the interview. I forewent my own way of thinking and followed suggestion.

As soon as I read their messages I immediately saw that part of my motivation had been my unconscious desire to create conflict in my peaceful life, not to mention my messianic belief that I can stitch together diverse political and social beliefs to create a utopian tapestry. Not really the kind of thinking you want guiding important life choices. In the past I would not have asked, if I had I may have still ignored the advice. By being open to suggestion, by letting go of my will in favour of the will of others, I begin to change. You can't think your way into acting differently, but you can act your way into thinking differently. I felt relieved to hand my autonomy over. This doesn't mean that in the future I won't engage with complicated political conversations, but by the time I do, I will be clearer about my own motivations and the likely consequences of my actions. A mentor will show you where you are on the path of your life and how to proceed along it. If you learn how to listen to your fear, how to recognize your uncertainty, you can then invite the superior consciousness of a mentor into your life. If you are unawakened, you will blithely stroll into more habitual anguish.

CHAPTER THIRTEEN

ANSWERING THE CALL

When I am doing a film in Ireland, am I really doing a film in Ireland? Or am I in a static tangle, like Christmas lights in the attic, knowing one bulb – but not which bulb – won't light. I am dealing with people and situations, which may or may not conform to the common consensual banner 'making a film in Ireland'. I could get fixated on anything. To what am I to tether my unblinking assessment of the external? Thankfully Nicola has come to do my hair and make-up but also to midwife me back and forth between the real and the unreal, my home and my family, the film set and the trailer, the cosmos of spilled interactions that could stain my day. If you work in entertainment you will be aware of the galling cliché of the actor who chums up to the crew with the unspoken, 'Yeah, I guess I'm just more at home with the horny-handed sons of the soil than with other pampered thesps' subtext; 'I guess it's because I'm a muthafuckin gangsta'. Well, I'm one of them. You should see me chatting football with me homies, eschewing the pleasures of the officers' mess to get down and dirty in the trenches. Comedy will always be my religion because so few things are just one thing and so many things are everything at once. This state of proletariat solidarity is both a cringey pose and entirely sincere. It is both a managed effort and completely who I am. I both entirely reject my childhood in Grays, Essex, and the fraught awfulness of my interactions with my shift-worker stepdad, not even – actually just my mum's live-in boyfriend – and entirely accept that I am, marrow deep, made there. I come from there, there where I never belonged.

Gary is one of the blokes who looks after the trailers, the trailers that make up base camp, where actors hang out, lights, kit and cables are stored, the production offices are located, toilets, food, the hub around which the set, where filming takes place, orbits. I chat to Gary about stuff. I chat to one of the other blokes on the crew, Ray, about BJJ and he hooks me up with a teacher nearby. Gary tells me one day about his sister, how her son, his nephew, died at eighteen from overdosing on a bad batch of MDMA. 'Would you talk to her?' he asks.

I see him every day over the course of the production and it is, all in all, a fairly typical experience. The usual blend of joy and boredom, unlikely moments in strange places. This is a kids' film and has child actors in it. They come with their own unique input. But, as with the *Mamma Mia* Immersive Dining Experience, the real trick is being present, not just in my head watching this stuff happen. On the last day of filming, after my Wonka-esque goodbye gift of ice creams has been administered with maximum potential disruption – in this case, me driving an ice cream van, siren blaring onto a live set and issuing sensitive child actors with sugar-laden desserts – I return to my trailer, content to be wrapping a film without having caused any unnecessary aggravation. Aside from the ice creams. Gary taps on the door. When I open it he already has his sister on the line.

I take the phone and close the door and the always slightly absurd ambience of the on-set trailer, in spite of my daft costume, immediately becomes calm and sacred. Kerry tells me that she is in Brent Cross shopping centre. 'Excuse me,' she says, and moves somewhere quiet. I sit down and picture her there. I breathe and prepare for her story. She is tentative and tearful for a few syllables, but propelled by tremulous certainty. 'James was a beautiful boy. More than my son he was my friend. So clever and sensitive. Not a druggy kid. He didn't do drugs a lot, I know he didn't. I didn't want him to go out that night. I wanted him to stay in. I wish I'd stopped him. I couldn't sleep, I kept looking at my phone. I had a bad feeling. At one fifty-eight I got a text, "I'm all right, Mum", at two fifty-eight I got another one from his phone saying "James is dead."' At this point the frequency, the intensity, the sharpness of tone changes, the grief is piercing and I try to fall backwards into purpose. 'My boy died on the street, Russell, on a pavement with three hundred people watching. Outside a club. He was dead by the time he got to the hospital.' I try to breathe and reach beyond my own lack of experience, my own inability to know something so profound and painful and source something useful. 'I'm getting grief counselling and they say I have to let go because the grief is going into my body and making me ill but I don't want to let go because I deserve it.' Then the terrible sound of a mother's pain.

I am not qualified to handle a mother's grief. I have no training in counselling or experience of this poignant and unanswerable despair. In this moment, though, I am on the phone to a grieving mother and the practical and rational limitations simply cannot be allowed to prevent me giving her the comfort and love her situation demands. William Blake did a series of engravings based on the Book of Job, rendering in immaculate tableaux Job's trials and suffering. It is as if Blake through his art and the Bible through the means of prose refer to the same subliminal truth, as if this story, the Book of Job, contains essential truths that we can only behold fleetingly and through the lens of image or language. In one tableau, Yaweh, or God, from on high shows Job 'the behemoth and the leviathan that I made, as I made thee'. These creatures as rendered by Blake are dreadful and uncanny. The dumb, muscular, skinless beast, all sinew and mouth. The deep-dwelling sea serpent ever present but invisible in its awful depths. When regarding these silently screaming images the horror of God's power is awesome, more terrifying though is the suggestion of ambivalence and that implicitly God the creator is not only good. In these images Job and Yaweh look the same, as if both the man made of flesh and the divine father are enshrined within a single form. These hypnotic tableaux induce a visionary state where we confront that God is within us and our own moral choices determine God's values. That the capacity for darkness and unconsciousness is as much part of the individual's psychological make-up as the inclination to love and kindness. That we have to be good because if we are not good then God is not good, that God's grace is realized through us and if we do not realize it then it does not exist. Like a terrible quantum equation where our intentions create all that is manifest. Do not be lost in the leviathan deep. Do not be trapped in the dumb carnality of form, transcend; transcend that God may imbue the world with his grace through you.

Knowing my own limitations I do not answer from myself. Knowing the hopelessness of such pitiless despair I do not attempt to placate with platitudes. I offer love. I offer this stranger, this woman that I am confronted with, the best of me, such as it is, in the hope that within me, within her, within us all, is the capacity to heal and be healed. There is no code in language, no silver bullet that can undo this pain but beyond language, beyond form, beyond death there is, there must be, connection. We cannot allow the universe to be unconsciousness and carnality, because we have the choice, because the possibility, the potentiality for love exists in all of us. Its existence as potential is also its demand for realization.

Aside from the love, comfort and forgiveness that anyone would offer a grieving mother I suggest that Kerry meets two of the mentors in this book, Manya and Meredith – healers, mothers, strong women who will be able to hold her pain for her until she is able to. I arrange for her to meet Liz Burton-Phillips, founder of DrugFAM, a charity that offers support to the bereaved relatives of drug users. We meet and attend a conference together in a Holiday Inn, so close to a roundabout you have to breathe in at the buffet. Liz set up DrugFAM when one of her twin sons died of a heroin overdose fourteen years ago. She has the cosy potency of a Harry Potter witch. She used to be a headmistress and has the easy authority that good ones have. Some people take the shock of trauma and somehow allow it to project their life in a new direction that seems to me to be about devotion, about serving others, about turning pain into love. At the conference people wear name tags that bear their own name and the name of the person they have lost. I suppose due to the nature of addiction, most of the attendees are parents. As the new father of two daughters I tiptoe through their grief with reverence and dread, knowing and not knowing the tears cried every time I meet someone else's eyes. I meet Kerry and Gary there. They are tawny-brown and unbowed people, attractive and sparky salt of the earth, good working-class people with fine values that have fought. Kerry I see for the first time and she is attractive and determined. Hardened by pain but still, thankfully, joyful.

We go into the conference and there are DrugFAM staff, mostly people that have previously used the service, and about 120 relatives and it's not easy to tell who has lost a relative twenty years ago and who is still in the full beam glare of recent bereavement. Liz has asked me to speak. There is a podium, a pull-down screen, round tables with tablecloths and bowls of not only Mars Celebrations but also Cadbury's Heroes on them. I am introduced by a long and unfussily kind, birch-like man called Peter, who I'd briefly engaged with in the corridor and ended up falteringly crying with. I cried, he didn't. I told him about a woman I know who'd lost her son twenty years ago when he was eighteen, through illness. She said of course that he was a lovely young man and how painful the process of his death had been. She said that her father had died recently, just a year ago, and recounted that after her son died, while still at the hospital, while the room was full to the ceiling with new anguish, her father had said to her, 'I am sorry. I am sorry that I brought you into this world to experience such suffering.' The words her father spoke, this awful apology, the agonized wish to undo all life because of the extremity of suffering, to rewind your own child's life because it inexorably led to unlivable sadness, scored me when I heard it. I told the tall man because of the context, because I was about to speak to people with comparable experience. It worked like a code on me as surely as if it were my pin number and I seeped self-pity.

From the podium I spoke from the perspective of an addict in recovery, alive not through any moral superiority but through luck and opportunity, neither of which their relatives were sufficiently granted. I told them, as Peter advised, that they could celebrate their relatives' lives without shame or stigma. I told them that my incessant prayer is that I will be spared the pain that they are living. But I know my children will die as all our children will die, that in prayer I just hope to negotiate the order of our departure. Let them become elderly sisters with well-lived lives, let them reach beyond the limits that have contained me, let them discover themselves and the beautiful world and how to connect to the permanent over the transient. Value integrity and honour over glory and pleasure. Kindness and truth over prestige and power. Let me as their father instil, or awaken, what they already seem, by their faces, to deeply and wordlessly know.

CONCLUSION

Your parents, God bless 'em, will take you as far as they can; your teachers will usher you as far as the institutions that employ them permit. But a mentor, well chosen, can guide you to the frontiers of your Self. Mentorship has been most successful in my life when I was simultaneously awakened to my need to change, willing to learn and there was an explicit and consensual method to pursue. Obvious examples from this book are as follows.

Chip Somers: I needed to get off drugs, he knew how to get off drugs using the 12 Step method. Or Chris Cleere, I wanted to learn Jiu Jitsu, he is a black belt in Jiu Jitsu from the Roger Gracie Academy. When you have the method and the master, your own willingness and surrender is all that is required for progress. More informal types of mentorship coalesce around friendship. Perhaps these less distinct examples are where there is no stated objective and there has been no overt request for help.

I would advise that in utilising this system and finding your own mentors, you look at your life and investigate where you would like to improve. Examine your existing friendships to see where there is the potential for greater learning. Who could you ask for further guidance in the areas where you feel you are deficient? Are you happy with your mental health? Your fitness? Your diet? Your marriage? 12 Step fellowships are an excellent entry point into a mentorship system and they are great for addressing most areas of emotional and spiritual deficiency, if you agree that most addictive behaviours are in some way compensatory.

In reviewing the mentors I have written about in this book, I demonstrate how you can replicate a wheel of guides, teachers and role models in your own life. Chip Somers, as I have said, mentored me out of chemical dependency, without which I would not have been able to even embark on a spiritual journey. I would've been trapped on an unconscious plain of circuitous self-harming.

As for Meredith, I never asked her to be a mentor but she is a person who so clearly operates on a spiritual frequency that even our earliest communications bore that timbre. She literally uses the I-Ching, an ancient fortune-telling system, not as part of her role as an acupuncturist but in her less formal but equally obvious guise as a wise woman.

Perhaps when we naturally migrate from the island of family, we unconsciously look out for tunes and codes that will nourish us. Perhaps somewhere in the infinity of our universe, in the limitlessness of our essential awakenedness, we have been each other's children, sisters, mothers, a thousand times. Maybe we hear in their voices the echoes of these endlessly resonating connections. There are more types of family than we can read in blood.

Jimmy was a very conscious, deliberate choice as a mentor and functions in my life as a symbol for my own aspirant manhood: 'I must be a father, a husband, a worker. I will have to face conflict. I will have to peel off the past and feel the rawness but move onward.' Ours is an unsentimental connection and highly functional in my life. I would never ignore Jimmy's counsel, never favour my own instinct above his. He offers experience rather than advice, and through conversation I deduce how his experience is applicable to my own circumstances. Because I asked Jimmy for help outright, our connection is as explicit and boundaried an example of mentorship as I can think of – like an apprenticeship.

Chris, on the other hand, is a teacher in a specific discipline and my relationship with him demonstrates how inner intention can elevate outer progress. Chris is not a 'romantic' or whimsical man, not one given to thinking about abstract ideas like mentorship, certainly not in grandiose or verbose terms. But through my attitude of total surrender and my openness to the potential life lessons learned in Jiu Jitsu, I have gained more from our relationship than I otherwise might have. Not that BJJ isn't steeped in ritual and tradition that for a soul like me are easy to poeticise; we line up before classes and bow; we clap to signal the start of new exercises; we run in a circle, ostensibly to warm up but it's basically a tribal dance; we all wear the same outfit. There's even a colour-coded belt system that is important across all interactions – not just sparring. The more I think about it, the more I see how these customs create a bonded community ambience.

Then there is Bruce. He is nominally a therapist, but he came to me through Jimmy. We share a philosophy and a camaraderie that has meant the relationship, while still boundaried, has exceeded the expected therapeutic limitations.

Like Bruce, Manya was a deliberate appointment to help with mental health too, and is now especially valuable in my marriage, in that she counsels my wife and gives both of us invaluable insight into how we are affecting one another.

On the more spiritual plane, there is Amma, who is considered a realization of divinity on Earth, which sounds like the very epitome of grand religiosity unless I consider it practically: what would it be to let go of all selfishness? To relinquish, to actually relinquish, my lust and greed? Who would I be if I lived by the Maharishi's blunt edict, 'Don't do what you know to be wrong, do what you know to be right'? Who would I be if every impulse to be kind, to say a kind word, to be loving was followed up? If I practised restraint when I knew that my words or thoughts or actions would hurt another? Would I become Christ? Or Amma or whatever prophet or avatar you admire? Is it possible? Is it less possible than what Gandhi achieved? Or what every grieving parent that chooses to go on with life achieves?

Why do we wait for extreme circumstances before reaching for extreme greatness? I heard 'The world does not require everyone to believe in God for its salvation, just for the people who do believe to start acting like it.' Can I become the man that God would have me be? What if I opened my heart to everyone, if I opened our home to the homeless, had the courage to outgrow my old program and reach into the unknown held only by the certainty of love. Well, for a start my wife would fucking kill me. She's pretty keen not to move strangers in with our babies, so I'm safe from that spiritual experiment for now. But a mentor like Amma provides a light for what may lie beyond the, let's face it, murky limitations of the modern, secular western life model.

During the heights of the garlanded Nuremberg, that rally of devotion on New Year's Eve, I noted Amma's admonishment of a keyboard player who was out of tune during the kirtan (a devotional song). She spoke to him assertively, not rudely, but it certainly wasn't wishy-washy. There are standards I thought, particularly when it comes to devotion. There is form. There is room to communicate with others sternly. I suppose you can't get hospitals and schools built on love alone, you need order, you need a plan, you need direction and we cannot flinch from discipline. After all, that is literally what is required of a disciple.

Whilst Amma seems to almost entirely inhabit an other-worldly realm, Radhanath Swami for me is a bridge to sainthood that I can conceive of crossing. Perhaps because I've now known him a long while, and I know he is from Chicago, and he speaks in the language of popular culture as well as the language of ancient India. He once said to my mother 'I love you very much and I see you as family, would you rather I was your son or your brother?' My mum, with her customary kindness said 'I cannot imagine being a mother to anyone other than Russell, so you can be my brother.'

Swamiji as he is known visited us when we were staying in Ireland. He ambled around film sets and comedy clubs with the same bemused luminescence he displays whenever I drag him somewhere odd. I distinctly remember his holy horror when we were (for some mad reason) at a lesbian rollerball event in LA. 'With your permission I would like to leave now' he said gently. Along with some of his devotees he came to my caravan on set in County Wicklow. My dad was there too with his girlfriend, Sandra. We sat crammed into the space, maybe eleven of us – me in the outrageous costume of a baddie in a kids' film. It went better than I expected in that it wasn't totally mental. Radhanath Swami elegantly told stories from the Bhagavad

Gita, about Krsna and Gujundra and all were absorbed. In part, I wondered how my volatile Dagenham dad with his no bullshit Del Boy intensity would take to this spiritual teacher. How would they find a common frequency? 'They're hardly gonna chat about West IIam,' I thought. But inner inquiry of this type was a disservice to them both. Ron Brand, of course, is a hugely inquisitive and intelligent man and was fascinated by the mystic. As the meeting resolved, Swamiji approached my dad and said with pure sincerity 'It is a great honour to meet you, you are a very beautiful man,' and I saw in real time how love can reach through any veneer and touch the truth within. I saw how my dad's rough carapace of sharp-elbowed hustle is what he uses to protect the child that lives in him, how love and kindness are the only vehicles that can cross the eerie silence between us and make real connections occur.

After a life of rejecting who I am and where I am from in order to survive and grow, I now see that I was born with everything I need. My mum with her cancer and car-crash vanquishing spirit and limitless love, and my dad – an intel-ligent, funny, tough and gentle working-class man – have been revealed to be the perfect parents for the man I have become. Like anyone on a quest – and we are all on a quest whether we accept it or not – I had to reject where I came from to become who I am, but with the neat efficiency that makes the genius of Campbell, Jung and Nietzsche bite, it is to home that I must return.

My mentors have helped to show me who I am, to accept who I am. A mentor baptises the child and invites the adult. A mentor teaches and demonstrates. If you feel that we live in a time that is defined by mean ugliness and ugly meaninglessness, then invite beauty and power into your life. Become willing to be taught, to connect to the invisible thread that runs between us all and that runs throughout all time, binding the empty space and filling it with love.

THE 12 STEPS

1

We admitted that we were powerless over our addiction,
that our lives had become unmanageable.

2

We came to believe that a Power greater than ourselves
could restore us to sanity.

3

We made a decision to turn our will and our lives over to
the care of God as we understood God.

4

We made a searching and fearless moral inventory
of ourselves.

5

We admitted to God, to ourselves and to another human
being the exact nature of our wrongs.

6

We were entirely ready to have God remove all these
defects of character.

7

We humbly asked God to remove our shortcomings.

8

We made a list of all persons we had harmed, and became willing to make amends to them all.

9

We made direct amends to such people wherever possible, except when to do so would injure them or others.

10

We continued to take personal inventory and when we were wrong promptly admitted it.

11

We sought through prayer and meditation to improve our conscious contact with God as we understood God, praying only for knowledge of God's will for us and the power to carry that out.

12

Having had a spiritual awakening as a result of these steps, we tried to carry this message to addicts, and to practise these principles in all our affairs.

OR, AS I WOULD HAVE IT:

1
Are you a bit fucked?

2
Could you not be fucked?

3
Are you, on your own, going to 'unfuck' yourself?

4
Write down all the things that are fucking you up or have
ever fucked you up and don't lie, or leave anything out.

5
Honestly tell someone trustworthy about how
fucked you are.

6
Well that's revealed a lot of fucked up patterns.
Do you want to stop it? Seriously?

7

Are you willing to live in a new way that's not all about you
and your previous, fucked up stuff? You have to.

8

Prepare to apologize to everyone for everything affected by
your being so fucked up.

9

Now apologize. Unless that would make things worse.

10

Watch out for fucked up thinking and behaviour and
be honest when it happens.

11

Stay connected to your new perspective.

12

Look at life less selfishly, be nice to everyone,
help people if you can.

ACKNOWLEDGEMENTS

Everyone at Bluebird.

Thank you Carole for your collusion and collaboration, your faith and good ideas, for helping me to create a series of books with consistent ideas.

Thank you Jodie for your innovative and passionate attitude to PR and promo, which can be, lets face it, a tricky business.

Laura, Alex and Hockley for your work on the book and the audiobook.

My team: Charlie and Jengo thank you for your brilliant work on this book. Thank you for letting me into your heads.

Other mentors who have aided me and my family: Tom and Beth Kerridge, you are great family role models, fine parents, lovely friends, great people.

Noel and Sara, Matt and Katie, Gee and Nadine, Karl and Rowan, couples, families, friends; thank God we don't have to do this alone.

Sharon and Nicola. As always.

James Ohene-Djan you have been a good mate for a long time, thank you.

Noel Fitzpatrick, thank you for the wizardry with our untenable animals and your example as a high functioning madman.

Bob Roth thank you for teaching me to meditate and for being a decent, beautiful, soulful brother on the path.

Deirdre and everyone at the David Lynch Foundation.

Noreen Oliver for being strong for the vulnerable.

Everyone at BAC O'Connor, Kendra, Tony.

Paul Busby and everyone at Genesis gym for creating a space for intensity and intimacy, friendship and competition. Ryron and Rener Gracie for the charismatic ass-kicking.

Jonathan Ross and Jane for being good and generous friends, for showing me the way in early days and staying tight when we were in a jam.

David and Wen Banks-Baddiel and Ez and Dolly for being a family we aspire to be like.

Sandipan and everyone in the Krsna consciousness movement for your support and kindness, for believing in the power of the unseen world.

Wednesday night brotherhood, my family of wounded soldiers, pirates, ne'er do wells and mystic lunatics.

Jason, always invaluable, incessantly beautiful.

Sy, reminding me to stay close to God.

Jeff, James, Perry. Thank you.

Emma Kenny, thank you for the guidance you have given us and the passion for play.

Jay and Kestrel for the Shamanic warmth and dream insights.

Debora thank you for taking such wonderful care of us.

Dear Dan for the soulful fitness.

Ian Rickson, gentle direction.

Bernard and Lesley. Thank you for being good grand-parents and for raising Laura to be such an extraordinary partner.

Laura, for everything.

And Mum and Dad, my first mentors, thank you for the love and determination.

ABOUT THE AUTHOR

RUSSELL BRAND IS a comedian and an addict. He's been addicted to drugs, sex, fame, money and power. Even now as a new father, sixteen years into recovery, he still writes about himself in the third person and that can't be healthy. He is the author of five books, including the *New York Times* bestseller *Recovery*. He still performs as a comic and is studying for an MA in Religion in Global Politics. He has two cats, two dogs, a wife, two daughters, ten chickens and sixty thousand bees in spite of being vegan curious. He is certain that the material world is an illusion but still keeps licking the walls of the hologram.